FROM EDEN TO EGYPT

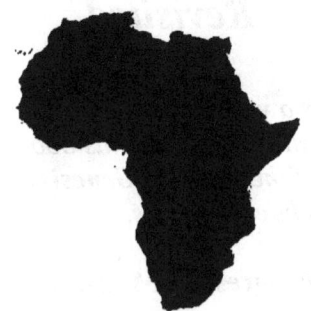

The Book of Genesis Revisited

Pastor Michael S. Williams, D.Min

The Juneteenth Publication Group

San Francisco, California

Resource *Publications*
An imprint of *Wipf and Stock Publishers*
199 West 8th Avenue • Eugene OR 97401

What Others Are Saying About, *From Eden to Egypt: The Book of Genesis Revisited*

*From **Eden to Egypt*** *is a wonderful piece of literature, and I think anyone who reads it will be blessed. This book will definitely give you a clearer picture of the **Book of Genesis**. God be praised for the Ministry of Dr. Michael Williams.*

Pastor R.E. Herrell, Progressive Ministry
San Jose, CA

*From **Eden to Egypt*** *is a challenging and insightful view of the **Book of Genesis**. Dr. Michael Williams moves us past the pedestrian interpretations of this book of creation. He masterfully weaves the various strands of our journey as a people, from the dawn of Creation in Africa to the glories of ancient Cush and Egypt in a provocative but easy to read manner. No Christian of African descent can claim to have a complete library without a copy of this book!*

Adumasa Adeyemi
Seminary Student, Berkeley, CA

The Garden of Eden in East Africa? Black Egyptians in Mexico 2,400 years before Columbus "discovered" America? I didn't know that! My understanding of the **Bible** *and Africa is greater now than ever!*

Mr. Timothy F. Albert, University Administrator
Houston, TX

I will never be able to look at the **Book of Genesis** *in the same way! Pastor Williams has done all Christians of African descent a tremendous service by writing this book! My walk with Christ, as well as my understanding of the important role Africans played in the History of Salvation, has been greatly enhanced!*

Ms. Cecelia Glover
Corporate Executive, Fremont, CA

Powerful! Moving! Insightful! Dr. Michael S. Williams' work reflects his zeal, reflection, and research in developing this vastly neglected and unexplored subject. He has cogently presented an intellectually stimulating relationship between our African forebears and the **Book of Genesis**. *By presenting the* **Biblical** *text with an Afrocentric perspective, he provides the tools that enable us to fathom the significant role that Africa and Africans played in the development of the ancient world.*

Rev. Floyd Bland, D.Min.
Not Of This World Ministries

The Juneteenth Publication Group
San Francisco

Published and Printed in the United States of America

© *Pastor Michael S. Williams, D.Min. 1999*

All rights reserved. No part of this publication may be reproduced, stored in a retrieval system, or transmitted, in any form or by any means, electronic, mechanical, photocopying, recording, or otherwise without the prior permission of The Juneteenth Publication Group.

This book is sold subject to the condition that it shall not, by way of trade or otherwise, be lent, re-sold, hired out or otherwise circulated without the publisher's prior consent in any form of binding or cover other than that in which it is published and without a similar condition including this condition being imposed upon the subsequent publisher.

Resource *Publications*
an imprint of Wipf and Stock Publishers
199 West 8th Avenue, Suite 3
Eugene, Oregon 97401

From Eden to Egypt
The Book of Genesis Revisited
By Williams, Michael S.
©2001 Williams, Michael S.
ISBN: 1-57910-680-3
Publication date: June, 2001
Previously published by , 2001.

This Book is Dedicated To The Sacred Memory of
Alberta "Mamo" Watson

1904-1997

and to

The Liberation of *Enslaved* **Knowledge**

TABLE OF CONTENTS

Foreword 8

A Word From A Friend And Colleague 9

Introduction 13

The Book of Genesis and Its Relationship to the Status of Africans in America 31

The Book of Genesis: Its Place in the Old Testament and its Relationship to Human Origins 59

Ham, His Descendants and Ancient Civilization 72

Egypt and Its "Time of Troubles" 89

Abraham's Family and Egypt's Hospitality 115

Where Do We Go From Here? 142

Appendix A 149

Appendix B 151

Appendix C 154

Appendix D 155

Appendix E 156

A Response to *From Eden to Egypt: The Book of Genesis Revisited*, by Rev. John Brinson, M.Div. 158

Foreword

I am deeply honored to pen words in praise of Dr. Michael S. Williams' seminal work. Anyone reading these leaves discerns rather quickly that tremendous time, thought, and research has gone into the writing of this sorely needed book. Dr. Williams has painstakingly revealed the relationship between our African forebears and **Genesis** with insight and *interpretive* skill. He remains true to the text, but with an Afrocentric perspective. Seldom in the life of one's seminary experience can one receive the *interpretive* insights shown by Dr. Williams. I am confident that this work will open new vistas of understanding to the serious reader of the **Biblical** record.

Another word needs to be shared. So much of what we receive in the African-American Church Community is through the oral tradition, save books of sermons. This pastor/preacher has given himself to serious study, research, and reflection so that we might be the recipients of work that will not only heighten our **Biblical** awareness but also allow us the opportunity to read particular **Biblical** narratives through the lens of our unique experience. This has been a monumental undertaking, and Dr. Michael Williams is to be lauded for a Job well done. This book will be around for years to come giving inspiration to all who seek crisp and clean understanding of the **Genesis** narrative so painstakingly outlined by this author.

Dr. Charles E. Booth, Pastor
Mt. Olivet Baptist Church
Columbus, Ohio
1999

A Word From A Friend And Colleague

The Reverend Dr. Michael Williams grew up in San Francisco's predominantly African American Fillmore District in the days immediately following the Second World War. In the mid-1960s, his family moved to San Francisco's predominantly African American Bayview Hunters Point Area. His pastor, the late Dr. Frederick Douglas Haynes, Sr., led (1932-1971) the oldest African American Baptist Church west of the Mississippi River, the Third Baptist Church of San Francisco. Dr. Haynes made it a point to expose his flock to African America's "movers and shakers." The late W.E.B. DuBois, Marian Anderson, Ethel Waters, Josephine Baker, Paul Roberson, and Congressman Adam Clayton Powell, Jr., lectured, sang, or addressed Third Baptist during his pastorate. Some of the most influential preachers of that era graced the pulpit of Third Church. Such pulpit giants as Gardner C. Taylor, T. M. Chambers, Sr. and National Baptist Convention, U.S.A President, J.H. Jackson visited "Third," as its members lovingly called it.

Dr. Haynes provided a forum for these African American luminaries, as well as a vehicle for his predominantly African American congregation's growth and awareness. The congregation, while boasting of many influential local African Americans, was made up predominantly of recent immigrants from America's rural American South. Some were recently discharged military service persons, some were shipyard workers; many of them worked on San Francisco's bustling waterfront. Like

Alberta Watson, Dr. Williams' grandmother, a sizable portion of the congregation happened to be "live-in" domestic workers. But, all benefited from Dr. Haynes' progressive vision. The author, Dr. Williams certainly did!

In the writing of this book, Dr. Williams continues the legacy of his late pastor in attempting to bring the "best" to his church and community. Dr. Williams' work, *From Eden to Egypt: The Book of Genesis Revisited,* is a stirring apologia for the centrality of an African cultural perspective in the *interpretation* of the Word of God. It is a profound rallying cry for re-thinking the place of Africans in the **Bible**. He exposes the ridiculous claims of Europeans regarding the presentation of the knowledge of God. He also lifts up African preachers and their authentic *interpretation* of the **Bible**. Dr. Williams also explores the problem that has bedeviled Human relations for at least 5,000-6,000 years—the role and place of persons of African ancestry on the world stage. He explodes any notion of African inferiority as an ingredient for social policy. The book is excellent in content, with an extremely readable style. Its structure provides helpful exegetical work on texts, strong summaries for each chapter, and exciting suggestions for additional investigation. I highly commend *From Eden to Egypt, The Book of Genesis Revisited* as an *interpretive* tool to pastors and laity alike.

Pastor James McCray
Jones Memorial United Methodist Church
San Francisco, CA

The Table of Nations With Reference To Noah and Ham
Genesis 9:18, 10: 6-19

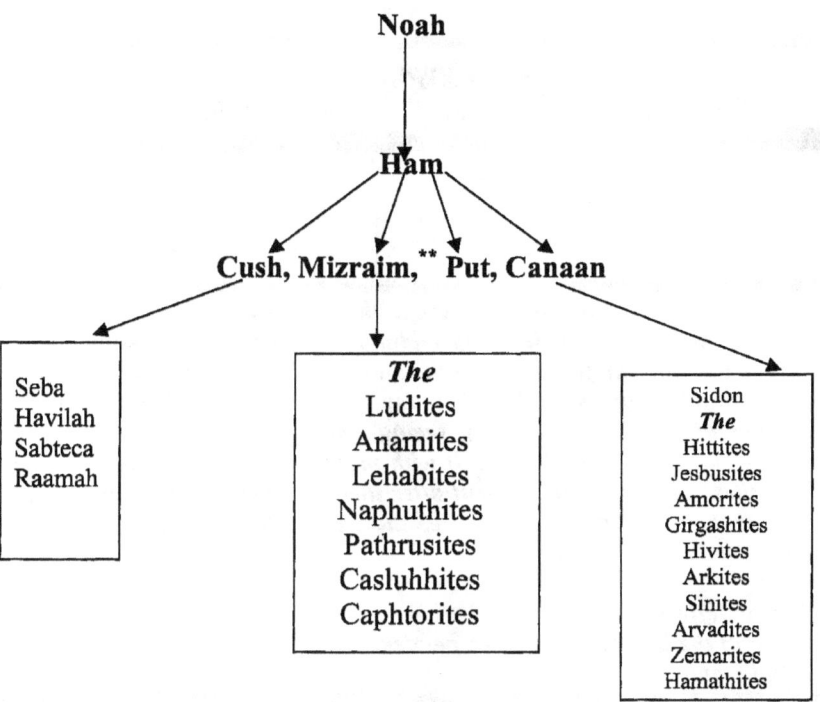

** **Mizaim** is also known as **Egypt**

> *"Envoys will come from Egypt,
> Cush will submit herself to God,"* Psalm 68: 31

> *"A Black, after hard labour through the day, will be induced by the slightest amusements to sit up till midnight, or later, though knowing he must be out with the first dawn of the morning. They are at least as brave, and more adventuresome. But this may perhaps proceed from a want of forethought, which prevents their seeing a danger till it be present. When present, they do not go through it with more coolness or steadiness than the whites. They are more ardent after their female: but love seems with them to be more an eager desire, than a tender delicate mixture of sentiment and sensation."*
>
> Thomas Jefferson
> Author of the Declaration of Independence and Third President of the United States

Introduction

All books have, or at least should have, a purpose. Actually, *From Eden to Egypt: The Book of Genesis Revisited* has several.

First, I am writing this book because my late grandmother, Alberta Watson, always encouraged me to express myself, especially with the printed word. Second, this book arises out of a seminar I led at the St. James Church, where I serve as Pastor. The seminar, conducted in the winter of 1997, was entitled *From Eden to Egypt: The Book of Genesis Revisited.*[1] The students were drawn from Saint James' young adult population. I thought it necessary to show them, in a systematic manner, the linkage between the *interpretation* of the **Bible** and their "status" as persons of African descent "existing" in America. I wanted to show how they exist in a society that is hostile to their very presence. This has been so since the arrival of their ancestors in Seventeenth Century Virginia. My point of departure was the so-called "curse" placed upon one of Noah's three sons, Ham (**Genesis 9:24-27**).

---

[1] A copy of the course outline is included in **Appendix A** on Page 151.

I chose this passage because Jews, Muslims, and Christians have used a distorted *interpretation* of this passage for the last 1,500 years as a weapon to enslave and oppress people of African descent. I also found it interesting that even though these groups do not accept each other's views of God; they have, to varying degrees, accepted the tradition of African "inferiority." This tradition arose from an interpretation of **Genesis 9:20-27** in the Fourth Century AD. Third, I obtained a college degree from the historically African[2] Bishop College, formerly of Dallas, Texas. I earned Masters and Doctoral degrees from Berkeley, California's world-renowned Pacific School of Religion. My educational experiences acquainted me with research methodology; this qualified me to make such an

---

[2]I am of the opinion that persons of African descent can never "do" enough to be allowed full participation in the American experience; therefore I do not consider them to be "Americans." I will refer to them, as well as Blacks of antiquity, as "Africans." This is not a very farfetched proposition. African slaves arriving in America's British colonies in the Seventeenth and Eighteenth Centuries were well aware of their "inferior" status. Therefore, they made it a point to acknowledge their unique heritage. They called themselves "Africans." Campbell notes that persons of African descent in this country, up until the mid-1820s and late 1830s, referred to themselves as "Africans," because the term "Negro" was equated with "slave." Hence, most Black institutions contained the word "African," in their title, e.g., The *African* Free Lodge, The *African* Methodist Episcopal Church, The Free *African* Society, etc. The name fell into disuse by the 1830s due to attempts on the part of powerful interests in the United States that sought to deport all "free" Africans to Africa. James T. Campbell, *Songs of Zion: The African Methodist Episcopal Church in the United States and South Africa* (New York: Oxford University Press, 1995), vii, 73. Also, Richard B. Moore, *The Name "Negro," Its Origin and Evil Use*, ed., W. Burghart Turner and Joyce Moore-Turner (Baltimore: Black Classics Press, 1992), 62.

attempt. Fourth, *From Eden to Egypt: The Book of Genesis Revisited* is in line with the recurring phrase in the prayers of some of my parishioners that states, "LORD, teach our pastor so that he may teach us."

I used the resources of modern scholarship throughout this book. I realize that many of my friends in the Academy will frown upon this book's aim and content. However, with all due respect, I did not write this book for the purpose of gaining their "acceptance," or even being taken seriously by them. I write as a pastor who seeks to service his congregation in the same way the Apostle Paul ministered to the Church at Corinth when he wrote, "for I have received of the Lord, that which I also pass onto you..."(**1 Corinthians 11:25**).

Lastly, as a person of African descent living in America, I see *dark* possibilities for our people in this country, especially as we face a new millenium. I purposely use the word *dark*, but not in the conventional sense. If I did, it would carry a negative meaning. I use *dark* in the positive sense. We are *dark* people, and our African ancestors were *dark*. Evidence shows that they were also the world's *first* Human Beings. Civilization, as we know it, is indebted to the Egyptian cities of Memphis and Thebes, and East Africa's Omo Valley more than it is to Athens and Rome.

My Audience

I want these pages to open a dialogue amongst common folk concerning the role Africans played in the drama of salvation as revealed in **Holy Scripture**. Who are the "common folk" of which I speak? They are a relatively mixed multitude, a "motley crew," if you will. They are the flotsam and jetsam of society located in America's so-called "inner cities," especially those sections that resemble my home, San Francisco's Bayview/Hunters Point area. The residents of these areas descended from Africans originally kidnapped from West Africa.[3] A few smoke crack, others are HIV+. Some take pride in living "on the edge." Some are living out their senior years alone in failing health, far away from the rural American South they left during and after World War II. Some of them do not attend church, but will tell anyone, from their arresting officer to the emergency room physician that, "Reverend Williams is *my* pastor, please call him." Some have been

---

[3] This study is crucial for persons of African descent living in the Americas and the Caribbean. There is a high probability they descended from ancient Black Egyptians. The late African Anthropologist Cheikh Anta Diop, drawing upon centuries-old traditions amongst West Africans, informs us they believed their ancestors originated in Egypt and migrated to West Africa. Diop says, " West African legends report that Blacks migrated from the east, from the region of the Great Water.... from what we know about the prehistory of the Nile Valley, we can legitimately assume that the 'Great Water,' is none other than the Nile." Cheikh Anta Diop, *The African Origin of Civilization: Myth or Reality*, trans. Mercer Cook (Chicago: Lawrence Hill Books, 1974), 179. In tandem with this suggestion, most persons of African descent living in North, South, and Central America, Mexico, Puerto Rico, the West Indies, Haiti, and Cuba are descended from slaves brought to those areas *from* West Africa.

brain washed to believe being shoved into the back of a police car, "Mirandized," booked, and arraigned is a natural way of life.

It is for this "crowd" I make this humble effort.

The Bible: Its Relationship With Africans in America

I believe in the ancient dictum that states, "history is written by the victors." In other words, those with superior resources will *interpret* any written document, whether it is the **Bible**, the law, or poetry, to their advantage. Furthermore, and perhaps this is my Baptist heritage emerging, the individual has the right, and even duty, to *interpret* the **Bible**, rather than to have it *interpreted* for him/her. To this end, I publish *From Eden to Egypt: The Book of Genesis Revisited* and encourage its use as an *interpretive* tool for the African experience in America.

The Role of Black Africa and The Holy Bible

Historically, Africa has been looked upon upon as the "Dark Continent." That phrase implies that its inhabitants are savages. A careful reading of the **Bible**, especially **Genesis**, will show this to be false. In order to get an idea of God's relationship with African people, we need not start at Yale Divinity School, Oxford University, Johns Hopkins University, The Massachusetts Institute of Technology, or Hieldelburg University. We can start in East Africa, where the Garden of Eden may have been located, and follow the stream of the text and see how it ends in Black African Egypt.

Many fine books and scholarly articles have been published on the subject of that African presence in the **Bible**. I will not try to duplicate their work. I am indebted to those whose knowledge of the African presence in the **Bible** dwarfs mine! The late AME Zion Bishop, the Right Reverend Alfred G. Dunston, Jr.,[4] Baptist pastor/scholar, Bishop William LaRue Dillard,[5] the Interdenominational Theological Center's Charles B. Copher,[6] the Reverend Walter Arthur McCray[7] and Howard University Divinity

---

[4] Bishop Alfred G. Dunston, *The Black Man in the Old Testament and its World* (Trenton, NJ: Africa World Press, Inc., 1992).

[5] William LaRue Dillard, ***Biblical** Ancestry Voyage: Revealing Facts of Significant Black Characters* (Morristown, NJ: Aaron Press, 1989).

[6] Charles B. Copher, "Three Thousand Years of **Biblical** Interpretation with Reference to Black Peoples," *Journal of the Interdenominational Theological Center* 13:1 (Fall 1985): 225-246. Also, Charles B. Copher, "The Black Man in the **Biblical** World," *Journal of the Interdenominational Theological Center*, 1:2 (Spring 1974): 7-16. Charles B. Copher, *Black **Biblical** Studies: An Anthology of Charles B. Copher, **Biblical** and Theological Issues on the Black Presence in the **Bible*** (Chicago: Black Light Fellowship, 1993).

[7] Rev. Walter Arthur McCray, *The Black Presence in the **Bible**: Discovering the Black and African Identity of **Biblical** Persons and Nations* (Chicago: Black Light Fellowship, 1990). Also, Rev. Walter Arthur McCray, *The Black Presence in the **Bible**, and the Table of Nations, With Emphasis on the Hamitic Genealogical Line from a Black Perspective* (Chicago: Black Light Fellowship, 1990).

School's Professor Cain Hope Felder[8] have contributed to our understanding of the African presence in the **Bible**.

However, though they expanded our understanding of the Black presence in the **Bible**, a sampling of articles and books written over the last 25 years, reveals only one article specifically dealing with the "curse" placed upon Ham.[9] I propose to examine this so-called "curse," by exploring its roots. To explore its "roots," it is necessary to look at the **Book of Genesis** in a different way. Therefore, I will concentrate on the **Book of Genesis** and relevant events in the first fifteen chapters of **Exodus**. I will draw upon resources from **Biblical** studies, history, science, and anthropology in order to make **Genesis** understandable.

---

[8]Cain Hope Felder, *Troubling **Biblical** Waters: Race, Class, and Family* (Maryknoll, NY: Orbis Books, 1989). I highly recommend Professor Felder's *Stony the Road We Trod: African-American **Biblical** Interpretation* (Minneapolis: Augsburg/Fortress Press, 1991). *Stony the Road We Trod* is a compilation of essays written by several of today's most influential **Biblical** scholars, Pastors, Systematic Theologians, and Ethicists of African descent on the subject of interpreting **Biblical** texts from an African-American perspective. Randell C. Bailey and Jacquelyn Grant recently published an extremely valuable collection of essays similar in scope and content to *Stony the Road We Trod*, entitled, *The Recovery of Black Presence in the **Bible**: an Interdisciplinary Exploration, Essays in Honor of Dr. Charles B. Copher* (Nashville: Abingdon Press, 1995).

[9]Gene Rice, "The Curse That Never Was (Genesis 9:18-27)," *Journal of Religious Thought* 29:1 (Spring/Summer 1972): 5-27. Other scholars have mentioned this "curse" in passing. But as far as I can ascertain, with the exception of Rice, no one has written an article or book with the "curse," as its specific subject.

My View

The **Book of Genesis**, while not a science text, preserves ancient traditions that hint at several points. First, Humanity originated on the continent of Africa. Second, Ham, Noah's second son, played a significant role in populating and civilizing the world. Third, Hamite civilization was compromised by attacks upon it by wandering savages originating in either the Pyrenees Mountain Range, nestled between southern France and northern Spain or in the Caucasus Mountain Range of Central Asia. These nomadic tribes migrated south sometime between 4400 BC and 4200 BC. Fourth, the Hamites played a decisive role in the History of Salvation. This History reaches its peak at the entrance of an empty tomb outside of the City of Jerusalem in AD 33, (**Matthew 28:1-8**).

Genesis: Reconstructing its Background

The way I make the **Book of Genesis** understandable is by attempting a *reconstruction* of what may have happened to the world's first civilizers, the Black Africans of Egypt and Cush. Whether it is a witness attempting to relay accurate answers to an attorney during a trial or a historian describing the attack on the American naval base at Pearl Harbor in 1941, both are trying to *reconstruct* what has *already* occurred. For example, no one knows the exact date when the Aryan tribes began migrating south from the Central Asia's Caucasus Mountain Range into the civilized world. Curtis suggests that they migrated in three waves. In his book, *Indo-European Origins*, he provides a provocative senario.[10]

From Eden to Egypt: The Book of Genesis Revisited, The "Curse" Upon Ham and the Arrival of the Northern Tribes

The general aim of *From Eden to Egypt: The Book of Genesis Revisited* is to shed new light on the damage caused to African people by the misrepresentation of the **Book of Genesis**. Specifically the so-called "curse" of Noah on his grandson, Canaan, will be addressed (**Genesis 9:24-27**).

I suggest that the invasion of Black Cushite civilization by wandering tribes spilling out of the Caucasus Mountain Range around 4400 BC began, what the late Chancellor Williams called, the "destruction of Black civilization." This set in motion events that eventually led to African people being regarded as "cursed."

I argue that far from being uncouth and unwashed savages who waited patiently for Europeans to *colonize*,

---

[10] According to Curtis, the Aryans or as they are sometimes called, "Indo-Europeans," or "Kurgans," began moving out of their place of origin, the Caucasus Mountain Range in Central Asia, in three waves. The migrations are thought to have occurred within the following time frames, 4400-4200 BC, 3400-3200 BC, and 3000-2800 BC. He is also wise to caution that it would be a mistake to take these dates too literally. V.R. Curtis, *Indo-European Origins*, American University Studies, Series XI, vol. 21 (New York: Peter Lang, 1988), 23.

civilize, convert, enslave, and in due course, *save* their "wretched Black souls," African people founded civilizations, sailed to the Americas before Columbus, and gave birth to what we call science. Far from being primitive cowering weaklings, as Hollywood would have us think, when African armies marched, the earth trembled. The ancient Black African did not live in blissful ignorance. To the contrary, great monuments of antiquity such as the Sphinx and the Pyramids rose on the fertile plains of northwest Africa due to the architectural skill and engineering genius of the Egyptians and the Cushites.

One of the more ridiculous claims of Europeans is that they were the first to present the knowledge of God to the poor inhabitants of the "Dark Continent," (Africa). Nothing could be further from the truth! As we will see, it was the *African* that passed on his knowledge of the Garden of Eden and creation to the Israelites.

Chapter Divisions

From Eden to Egypt: The Book of Genesis Revisited is divided into six chapters. **Chapter 1** presents my theory of how Western Europeans unleashed terror and destruction upon persons of African descent by *misinterpreting* **Genesis 9:18-27**. Despite the myth that African people in the New World simply accepted their "master's" *interpretation* of the "curse," history informs us, they struggled to provide their own *interpretation* of the **Bible**. This *interpretation* ran contrary to the *interpretations* given to them. The enslaved Africans saw the God of the **Bible** as being their *liberator*, not their *enslaver*. I will close **Chapter 1** by suggesting that the belief in Ham's children's "inferiority" is so deeply ingrained in the social attitudes towards African peoples that, even though the **Biblical** story of the "curse" is not generally known, its effects can still be felt.

Chapter 2 explores the **Book of Genesis'** place in the **Old Testament**, and its relationship to the origin of Humanity.

Chapter 3 looks at the role Ham's descendants played in populating and civilizing the world.

Chapter 4 gives a summary of the Egyptian/Cushite world's life and death struggle against the northern tribes. More precisely, **Chapter 4** will explore the tremendous amount of social upheaval and carnage in the ancient world beginning with advances made by migrating tribes from the frigid climes of Central Asia's Caucasus Mountain Range, around 4400-3000 BC. The migration of the white Caucasus tribes set the stage for the belief that *Black* was *evil* and *white* was *good*. This belief set the stage for the misrepresentation of Noah's "curse" upon Ham, which was nothing more than an angry outburst aimed at his grandson, Canaan (**Genesis 9:20-25**). The misrepresentation of Noah's "curse" upon Ham provided the excuse for the pillaging of Africa that began in earnest with the Trans-Atlantic Slave trade in the 1600s AD.

Chapter 5 will comment on the relationship of the Patriarchs, Abraham, Isaac, Jacob, Joseph, etc., to Egypt, and in due course, the History of Salvation.

Chapter 6 will raise questions for reflection and summarize the book.

Assumptions

No one begins any study without basic assumptions. I must be honest; I am not free from them. My first assumption is—the **Bible** is the inspired **Word of God**. However, it can be *interpreted* in such a way so as to liberate or enslave people, specifically Africans. Second, I believe Humanity originated in Africa. I derive this belief from a large body of scientific, **Biblical**, and African beliefs. If this is so, it suggests that the first Human Beings were Black-skinned. Evidence also suggests that these people colonized and civilized the world. The evidence I present could be *interpreted* in such a way as to "prove" Black-skinned people are "superior." Nothing could be further from the truth. As Diop reminds us,

> There is no particular glory about the cradle of Humanity being in Africa, because it was just an accident. If the physical conditions of the planet had been otherwise, the origin of Humanity would have been different.[11]

---

[11] Cheikh Anta Diop, *Civilization or Barbarism: An Authentic Anthropology*, trans. Yaa-Lengi Meema Nyemi (Chicago: Lawrence Hill, 1991), 16. Finch points out, "[t]he African race, once inhabiting the cultural pinnacle of the world, now seems to occupy the "lowest" rung among the world's communities. Such are the forces of history and the workings of

History shows that the *interpretation* of events, traditions, or in our case written documents, can pit one group *against* another. This is especially true when it comes to the issue of skin-color and such issues as "racial purity."

Third, I will admit that the idea of the entire Human family originating with a single couple (**Genesis 4-5**), or the earth being repopulated by a single family (**Genesis 10-11**) may not hold up under the withering gaze of scientific inquiry. It is not my task to argue those points. Someone else must do that. Rather than argue for the existence of an actual Adam and Eve, or a Noahic family grouping, I say it is up to the *reader* to decide. Adam and Eve, Noah, Shem, Japheth, Ham, Cush, Egypt, Canaan, etc. could be viewed

---

fate....*nature cares nothing for races per se.* In fact, gene pools act in such a way as to ensure their own survival; some prevail, others pass away. Thus all the races that exist today are contingent upon proven adaptability; nothing more, nothing less. [Italics added]. Charles S. Finch III, M.D., *Echoes of the Old Darkland: Themes from the African Eden* (Decatur, GA: Khenti, Inc. 1992), 28. J.A. Rogers wisely put the issue of "race" into perspective when he suggested that "racism," the thought that one group is superior to another, is a modern phenomenon. He pointed out that it was ridiculous. After all, he noted, various white groups are divided amongst themselves as to which is the "greatest." During World War II, he wrote, "[t]he battle for racial supremacy is now on. Superior Anglo-Saxon [White Britons and White North Americans] versus super-superior Aryans [Germans]....[f]or centuries the Anglo-Saxon had proclaimed himself [racially pure and superior]. But now the Hitler Aryan has announced that he is 'the master race, destined to rule the world.' He is looking down on the Anglo-Saxon much as how the latter looked down on the [African]. In a word, he is calling the Anglo-Saxon 'nigger.' " J.A. Rogers, *Sex and Race: Negro-Caucasian Mixing in All Ages and in All Lands*, Vol. 1, *The Old World*. (St. Petersburg, FL: Helga Rogers, 1967), 7.

symbolically, or *literally*. For my purposes, I view them *textually*. In other words, these characters appear in the **Biblical** *text*. Their importance, or lack thereof, has caused one portion of the Human Race to be viewed in a negative context based upon the *interpretation* of a given *text*. Also, this does not preclude ancient Hamite, Canaanite, Egyptian, etc., populations from having *their own* understanding or traditions as to how their families, clans, tribes, or nations began. What *their* self-understanding was, if we are able to ever get a complete picture of it, may run contrary to *Western* methods of historiography. Perhaps *they* felt they descended from a single individual, maybe *they* did not. But how they viewed their origins—or how *we* view those origins—are of little importance for this study. However, for the sake of simplicity, I will personify the population groups as if they were actual people. Therefore when I speak of Ham, Cush, Canaan, etc., I represent that the *populations* identified with those *particular names* rose to greatness, declined, and fell. In other words, I will speak as if a national group sprang from one person. *Historically*, however, I see the Patriarchs, Abraham, Isaac, and Jacob as actual individuals. There is no valid reason to see them otherwise.[12]

Fourth, African people in the United States live in a society hostile to their very presence. Therefore, *nothing*

---

[12] Soggin categorically rejects the idea that the Patriarchs (Abraham, Isaac, Jacob, Joseph, etc.) were actual persons. He offers a well crafted, but non-convincing argument against their actual existence. J. Alberto Soggin, *A History of Ancient Israel*, trans. John Bowen (Philadelphia: The Westminster Press, 1984), 89-108.

they can ever do will allow them to be full participants in the American experience.

Fifth, I deliberately choose not to use the Egyptian dating arrangement that dates back to the time of Manetho. Manetho was the great Egyptian priest/historian, who lived during the so-called "Greek Period" of Egypt's history (c. 320-c.31 BC). Manetho chronicled Egypt's history by dividing it into 30 "Dynasties." The dating for these groupings generally range from 2920-332 BC. Some Dynasties, like the Twenty-Fifth, are generally thought to be Cushite, i.e., Black African. However, I contend that even if the ruling houses or dynasties are *not called* Cushite or Black by Manetho, according to contemporary American custom (*this relates to the so-called "one drop of African blood rule,"*) those dynasties, to say nothing of the Egyptian people themselves, should be considered *Black*. This could also explain why many of ancient Egypt's rulers and subjects looked anything *but* African.

Reading Aids

So as to facilitate a quick reading of this book, I have tried to make it "user friendly." I did this in three ways. First, I chose to use "footnotes" and not "endnotes." Personally, I find it annoying to read a book, see an interesting reference, and have to go to the back of the book to check it. My method of using footnotes will allow you to go directly to the bottom of the page and read my reference notes. Second, there may also be a reference not found in the footnote that could be of interest to you. In such a case,

I placed supplementary readings at the end of each chapter under the heading, *Suggestions for Further Reading*. Third, this book should be read in conjunction with the **Bible**. Some readers may question whether this book is "*Afro*centric," I believe it is. However, I would argue that it is also "***Biblio*centric**." I encourage you to **READ** the **Bible** in conjunction with this book. To help you in this area, all words related to the **Bible**, i.e., books of the **Bible** and the adjective "**Biblically**" are all in **BOLD** face type. This should help, especially for those readers that are not familiar with the **Bible**.

Personal Thanks

I would have never been able to write *From Eden to Egypt: The Book of Genesis Revisited,* without support. Intellectual stimulus came from many people. I am indebted to them. The Ministerial Brotherhood of the Bay Area Baptist District Association, District Moderator T.P. Fields, and my faculty colleagues at the Southern Marin Bible Institute, under the leadership of its visionary leader and founder Dr. Emmanuel Akognon, a fertile "space" for my thinking process. There are some preacher/pastors that have pushed me to think. A few of these colleagues are: Amos Brown, Phillip Drummer, Charlie Crier, Bishop James Adams, Jimmie Hardaway, Steven Bailey, Mervin Redmond, Milton H. Williams, Dorri Anderson, Governor Johnson, Shad Reddick, and Wenzell Jackson all of San Francisco and H.L. Garnett, of Oakland, California. H. Bernard Branch of Virginia, Charles Thomas of Baltimore, and Past Moderator R.K. Gordon of the Home and Foreign Mission District Association encouraged me.

I have sat at the feet of some of the greatest scholars of our time. They are as follows, Pacific School of Religion's Old Testament Professor, John H. Otwell, now of Blessed Memory, Professor John D. Mangram, formerly of Bishop College, Dallas, Texas, now of Jarvis Christian College of Hawkins, Texas; Professors Cain Hope Felder and Evans Crawford both of Howard University Divinity School in Washington, DC and Professor Gayraud Wilmore, formerly of Atlanta's Interdenominational Theological Center. I had the assistance of one of the finest copy editors to be found anywhere, Mrs. Tara Evans Bell. In the area of intellectual property matters, the assistance of Attorney James Li, of the San Francisco office of Sedgwick Detert Moran and Arnold, proved invaluable. Moral support came from my wife, Patricia.

Bibliographic support came from Rev. John Brinson. Not only is Rev. Brinson a friend of over 20 years, but he is a fount of knowledge when it comes to the role of Africans in the ancient world. I would like to say in closing—**TO GOD BE THE GLORY!**

Pastor Michael Shelly Williams, D.Min.
Juneteenth 1999
Bayview/Hunters Point
San Francisco, California

"David sent written instructions to his field commander, Joab. He sent the instructions by Uriah. In the letter were the following instructions: seek out the most dangerous section of the battlefield. Make sure that Uriah is sent there. Then withdraw all of the soldiers—except Uriah. I want to make sure that he does not return alive." 2 Samuel 11-15

"Joab had the city surrounded. No one could get in or out. He made sure that Uriah was in an exposed position. The men of the city rushed out and fought the Israelites. Some of the Israelites were killed—one of the slain was Uriah the Hittite." 2 Samuel 11: 16-17

Chapter 1
The Book of Genesis and Its Relationship to the Status of Africans in America

1.1 The Power of Writing and Interpreting

Pablo Richards said, "a text without history is a text that does not make history."[1] This statement is problematic. How can a text, a written document, *make* history? *Written documents* do not *make* history. *Human Beings have* the power to *make* history after they have *read* and *interpreted written documents*, and in due course, decide to *act* upon what they have *read*. For instance, the person that receives a "Dear John" or "Dear Jane" letter *reads* it and weighs his or her options. The recipient can *interpret* the letter as a sign that the sender was not worth their while, throw the letter in the trash, forget about the sender, and move on. Or the reader can *interpret* the letter as a personal rejection and attempt homicide or suicide.

This is true when it comes to the status of Africans in America. A prime example of this is the way the United States Constitution was *written* and then *interpreted* in reference to Africans. The American Constitution stands as one of the greatest *written* documents produced by Western

---

[1] Pablo Richard, *La fuerza espiritual de la iglesia de los pobres* (San Jose, Costa Rica: D.E.I., 1987), 116; quoted in Robert and Mary Coote, *Power, Politics and the Making of the **Bible*** (Minneapolis: Augsburg/Fortress Press, 1990), v.

society. As a *written* document, it was harmless even though it gave Africans the "status" of 3/5 of a Human being.² However, since the Constitution is the foundational document from whence "rights" and "liberties" spring in American society, the 3/5 issue has historically caused Africans to be effected in a negative way.

Many Africans ignore the fact that the United States Constitution was *not* written with *their well being in mind*. An excellent example of this type of thinking is "conservative" African Supreme Court Justice Clarence Thomas.

The late African Federal Court of Appeals Justice, A. Leon Higginbotham wrote,

> My daughter suggests the following (she has a Ph.D. in clinical psychology.) She says Clarence Thomas must think that had he been living in 1776 he would have been a

---

²During the debates surrounding the adoption of the Federal Constitution (1787), it was decided to distribute the number of seats in the lower chamber of the Congress, the House of Representatives, based on census data. In order to boost the South's population figures, African slaves were considered 3/5 of a Human Being. This would keep the more populous Northern states from overwhelming the sparsely populated Southern states in the House of Representatives. This would also allow the Southern states to increase their population figures, and at the same time retain their tradition of keeping African people in a less than Human status. Fred Taylor Wilson, *Our Constitution and its Makers* (New York: Fleming H. Revel, 1937), 98. Also, Staughton Lynd, *Class Conflict, Slavery, and the United States Constitution: Ten Essays* (New York: The Bobbs-Merrill Company, 1967), 185-213.

> confidant of Thomas Jefferson, or if he were living in 1787, he would have been a confidant of James Madison....Thomas never considered that in all probability he would have been Jefferson's or Madison's *slave*[!] We must always recognize the historic fact that despite all the good things Jefferson, Madison, and those others did; [Africans] were in a status called *slavery* when the Constitution was drafted. [Italics Added].[3]

A good example of Higginbotham's point was an *interpretation* of the Constitution in a decision handed down in 1856 by the U.S. Supreme Court in the infamous case of *Dred Scott v. Sanford*. United States Supreme Court Chief Justice Roger Brooke Taney, writing for the majority of his fellow justices, penned these words,

> [Africans] are altogether *unfit* to associate with the white race, either in social or political relations, and so far inferior that [Africans] have no rights that a white man is bound to respect, and that [an African] might be justly and lawfully. ... reduced to slavery for *his* benefit. [Italics Added][4]

---

[3] A. Leon Higginbotham, Jr. "Opening Argument," in Linn Washington, ed., *Black Judges on Justice: Perspectives from the Bench* (New York: The Free Press, 1994), 6.

[4] Paul Finkelman, *Slavery in the Courtroom* (Washington DC: Library of Congress, 1985), 44, 46-48.

Twentieth Century Europe witnessed the negative impact of reading, *interpreting*, and acting upon a written text. Adolf Hitler, while serving a prison sentence in Bavaria's Landsberg Prison for his part in a failed revolt in 1923 against the Bavarian government, wrote *Mien Kampf*, (My Struggle). *Mien Kampf* contained a 25-point program which, among other things, called for the extermination of the world's Jewish population and the conquest of Europe.[5] When his Nazi party came to power in Germany in 1932, his followers acted on his program. Seven years later, Germany invaded Poland and World War II began.

1.2 The Negative Effects of Racist Biblical Interpretation And Noah's "Curse" Upon Ham

The *interpretation* of **Biblical** texts has had a profoundly negative effect upon African people. This negative effect predates the arrival of Africans in the British colony of Virginia as "bond servants" in 1619[6] by at

---

[5] John Toland, *Adolf Hitler* (New York: Ballantine Books, 1976), 301.

[6] Contrary to popular belief, the first Africans to arrive in the British colony of Virginia in 1619 were *not* slaves. They were considered "bond servants." They were to serve as laborers on plantations for a specified number of years and then be released. They, like their white counter parts, were bound to plantation owners for the sole purpose of planting, cultivating and harvesting agricultural produce. However, the demands for the produce outstripped the supply of available bondservants. To remedy this, bond servitude degenerated to "slavery" based upon skin color. By the middle 1600s, Africans began to be considered *property*, and became *slaves* for life. John Hope Franklin, *From Slavery to Freedom: A History of Negro Americans* (Alfred A. Knopf. 1974), 56-60.

least 1,300 years. The "science" of *interpreting* the **Bible** is called hermeneutics.[7] Basically, hermeneutics seeks to read a **Biblical** text and *interpret* it for the present.

One of the most notorious examples of distorted hermeneutics is found in the *interpretation* of **Genesis 9:20-21.** A summary of the text goes as follows:

- **9:20,** Noah planted a grape orchard.

- **9:21,** He produced wine from the grapes. He drank some of the wine. He became drunk and apparently "passed out" naked in his tent.

- **9:22,** One of his sons, Ham, happened upon his father in a drunken state and informed his siblings about it.

- **9:23,** Noah's other sons, Shem and Japheth, instead of looking directly at their naked father, covered him with an article of clothing.

- **9: 25-27,** After Noah awakened and found out that Ham gazed upon him while in a drunken stupor, he

---

[7]Clyde T. Francisco, *Introducing the Old Testament* (Nashville: Broadman Press, 1977), 44. A twisting of the **SCRIPTURES,** based upon faulty hermeneutics, caused white women with mental problems to be branded as "witches," and in due course burned alive in colonial Massachusetts during the 1600s. James D. Smart, *The Strange Silence of the **Bible** in the Church: A Study in Hermeneutics* (Philadelphia: Westminster Press, 1970), 92.

placed a curse upon Canaan, Ham's son. He cursed him by stating that Canaan, Ham's son, would be a slave to his brothers.

Negative *interpretations* of this text in regards to African people began to appear as early as AD 200-600 in Jewish Rabbinical commentaries on the **Scriptures**. Three[8] of these *interpretations* are especially notorious. Two of them are relevant to our discussion. The first comes from *Midrash Rabbah-Genesis XXXVI: 7-8,*

> R[abbi] Huna said in R[abbi] Joseph's name: (Noah declared), "You have prevented me from begetting a fourth son, therefore I will curse your fourth son. R[abbi] Huna also said in R[abbi] Joseph's name: you have prevented me from doing something in the *dark* (sexual relations with his, i.e., Noah's wife), therefore your [descendants] will be *ugly* and *dark skinned*." R[abbi] Hiyya said: "Ham and the dog [had sexual relations with their partners] on the ark, therefore Ham came forth *Black*-skinned while the dog publicly exposes its copulation [Italics Added].[9]

---

[8]*Midrash Rabbah, Genesis*, ed., Rabbi Dr. Isidore Epstein (London: The Socino Press, 1939), Chapter xxxvi, 7-8, 293, in Copher, "Three Thousand Years of **Biblical** Interpretation," 231.

[9]ibid., 232

A strange *interpretation* indeed! It appears that Noah extends the curse because Ham prevented him from engaging in sexual relations with his wife. **Genesis 9:20-21** does *not* mention this.

The second reference from early Rabbinical writings comes from the *Tanhuma Noah 13, 15*. In a fit of anger, Noah curses Ham by saying,

> "...because you twisted your head around to see my nakedness, your grandchildren's *hair* shall be *twisted* into *kinks*, and their *eyes red;* again because your *lips* jested at my misfortune, [your descendant]'s [lips] shall *swell;* and because you neglected my nakedness, [your *descendants*] shall go *naked*, and their [*male sex organs*] shall be shamefully *elongated. The men of this race are called Negroes.*" [Italics Added] [10]

The second Rabbinical *interpretation* of **Genesis 9:20-22** elaborates on the text by showing African physical characteristics as being a result of the "curse." It is obvious that the Rabbis took extreme liberties in *interpreting* the **Biblical** text and identifying certain physical characteristics, e.g., skin color, hair texture, male genitalia, and lip size of African people with Noah's "curse."

The identification of Africans and Noah's "curse" laid the groundwork for negative views by other religious

---

[10] ibid.

movements toward Ham's descendants. Although the Muslim holy book, the *Koran*, does not contain any explicit views concerning African people, the early followers of Mohammed borrowed heavily from prevailing Jewish teachings. This caused them to rationalize the low status of conquered African people in their midst.[11] How ironic! Noah *did not* curse Ham! In a fit of anger, perhaps nurtured by a "hang over," he cursed *Canaan*!

As **Proverbs 23: 29-30, 33-35** instructs us, an intoxicated person:

---

[11]According to Hood, the Arab's views of the African were influenced by three factors. First, non-Koranic writings concerning Ham. Second, their conquest of certain parts of Africa gave them a sense of superiority over subjected Africans. Third, coming into contact with light-skinned civilizations of Asia also influenced their negative view of Africans. This caused them to negatively contrast fair-skinned people with Africans. Robert E. Hood, *Begrimed and Black: Christian Traditions on Blacks and Blackness* (Minneapolis: Augsburg/Fortress Press, 1994), 9. One of the greatest slave revolts in history occurred in the 9th Century AD. It involved East African slaves, as well as soldiers that had been kidnapped from East Africa. They were taken to the Arab dominated Abbasid Empire. Arab slave traders kidnapped the Africans, called the "Zanj," a Persian word, for "Negro." The word "Zanj" combined with the Hindu word "Bar" is where we get the name for the island lying off the Eastern Coast of Africa named "Zanzibar." Zanzibar literally means "country of the Black Man." Alexandre Popovic, *The Revolt of the African Slaves in the 3rd/9th Century*, trans. Leon King (Princeton, NJ: Markus Wiener Publishers, 1999), 14-15. That empire occupied the area now known as Iraq. The Africans worked their Arab master's plantations and salt mines under harsh and brutal conditions. The "Zanj," rose up against their Arab captors and military superiors. They were led by an African slave, a certain 'Ali b. Muhammad. He has been compared to Rome's Spartacus and Haiti's Toussant L'Ouverture. The bloody revolt raged on for fourteen years (AD 869-883) until Imperial forces crushed it. Also see, Copher, "3000 Years of **Biblical** Interpretation," 235, 238.

- Will always have problems, needless bruises, and bloodshot eyes **(23: 29-30)**
- Will hallucinate **(23: 33)**
- Will be likened unto a person "sleeping one off" on top of a ship's mast **(23: 34)**
- Will be able to be beaten, punched and kicked, without feeling a thing! **(23: 35)**

After doing a careful analysis of **Genesis 9:18-27**, Gene Rice called the passage in question, the "curse that *never* was."[12] If this "curse" never existed, then it would have to have been literally "pulled out of thin air" by persons predisposed to classify African persons as less than Human.

The view of Ham as being "cursed" by Noah served as an underpinning for American enslavement of Africans, from the colonial period[13] up to the Civil War. On the eve of the American Civil War, John H. Hopkins, the Episcopal Bishop of Vermont, wrote,

> The first appearance of slavery in the **Bible** is the *Wonderful* [?] prediction of the patriarch Noah **(Genesis 9:25)**...the

---

[12] Rice, "The Curse That Never Was," 5-6

[13] Hood, *Begrimed and Black*, 59-60.

Almighty, foreseeing the total degradation [of African people], ordained them to servitude...and all history proves how accurately the prediction has been accomplished even to this *present day*. [Italics Added] [14]

1.3 African Counter-Interpretations

As Africans began to arrive in Britain's American colonies during the mid-1600s, they were exposed to the "curse" of Ham as a way of brainwashing them into believing their "status" as slaves had been ordained by God. The majority of the slaves brought to these shores rejected this *interpretation* of the **Bible** and, as James T. Campbell put it, "began the long process of making the Gospel their own."[15]

---

[14] The Society for the Diffusion of Political Knowledge, *The Bible View of Slavery* (New York: The Society for the Diffusion of Political Knowledge, 1861), 118. An earlier example of *misinterpretation* as well as misapplication of the **Bible** is contained in a letter written to a colonial judge in 1701 by a slaveholder, John Saffin. In the letter, he justified the institution of slavery in colonial Virginia partially on **Biblical** grounds. Saffin gave a two-fold justification of slavery. According to Saffin, slavery was justified because, a) based upon his reading of **Genesis 9:25-27**, it was divinely ordained, b) the Gospel could be presented to Africans while in slavery, and Abraham brought slaves with money, **Genesis 14:14**. "John Saffin: A Reply to Judge Sewall," quoted in Louis Ruchames, ed., *Racial Thought in America From the Puritans to Abraham Lincoln* (Amherst, MA: The University of Massachusetts Press, 1969), 56-57. Also, Joseph Boskin, "The Origin of American Slavery: Education as an Index of Early Differentiation," *Journal of Negro Education* 35(Spring 1966): 12.

[15] Campbell, *Songs of Zion*, 3.

The Africans did *not see* themselves as pitiful victims. They identified with the trials and tribulations of various **Biblical** characters.[16] In fact, the line between their circumstance and actual **Biblical** times would disappear in the midst of their religious services, especially when they would identify with the Children of Israel. Raboteau notes,

> It is hard to exaggerate the intensity of the [African Slave's] identification with the children of Israel...[for the slaves], **Exodus** became dramatically real. Sermons, prayers, and songs reenacted the story. [They identified] with the Hebrews, they traveled dry-shod through the Red Sea; they too saw Pharaoh's army 'get drownded;' they stood beside Moses on Mount Pisgah and gazed over into the Promised Land; they crossed the Jordan under Joshua and marched with him around the walls of Jehicho.[17]

---

[16] Raboteau pointed out that the slaves often compared their struggles with those experienced by such **Biblical** characters as Jacob, Moses, Noah, Daniel, "Weeping Mary," "Sinking Peter," and "Doubting Thomas." Albert J. Raboteau, *Slave Religion: The Invisible Institution in the Antebellum South* (New York: Oxford University Press, 1978), 250-251.

[17] Raboteau says, "Slave owners...were well aware that the **Exodus** story could be a source of unflattering and even subversive analogies. It took no genius to identify Pharaoh's army in the slave songs, "My army cross over/ o'Pharaoh's army drowned." ibid. According to Duitsman-Cornelius, an early Nineteenth Century South Carolina state senator, Whitemarsh Seabrook, led a vigorous campaign to eradicate *all* forms of education for Africans, both slave as well as "free," in that state during the 1820s and 1830s. He felt education for the African should be limited to knowing that he was bound to his owner by the laws of God and of Man, "and that no

The slaves went so far as to identify various areas of the United States and Canada with those of the **Bible**. The slave-holding states were considered "Egypt," and the "free" states, along with Canada, were considered "The Promised Land."[18]

1.4 African Slaves and the Quest for Biblical Literacy

Since the *interpretation* of the **Bible** had a direct relation to their social status, the slaves had an intense desire to learn how to read. Literacy, freedom, and the **Bible** went hand in hand. The slave that learned to read had an unspoken duty to "take the **Bible** back"[19] to his or her fellow slaves. Once this was done, the slaves could learn for themselves what the text *said* instead of relying upon the *interpretations* of their "masters."

Human authority can sever the link that unites them." He also felt that religion and literacy was a dangerous combination, and that any one that wanted to introduce the slave with the *entire* **Bible** was "fit for a room in the lunatic asylum." In other words, he understood that although the **Bible** contained passages that appeared to sanction slavery, it contained portions that were irreconcilable with the practice. Janet Duitsman-Cornelius, *When I can Read My Title Clear: Slavery and Religion in the American South* (Charleston, SC: University of South Carolina Press, 1991), 86. Also, Vincent L. Wimbush, in Felder, *Stony the Road We Trod*, 85-86.

[18] ibid.

[19] Duitsman-Cornelius, *"When I Can Read My Title Clear*, 86.

The linkage between literacy, the **Bible**, and freedom was not lost upon their enslavers. Punishment would be swiftly meted out upon a slave that learned to read. The punishment could come in one of three forms. The "guilty" slave could have a body part cut off, whipped almost to death, or executed.[20] The slaves were well aware of the hazards of learning to read, but even death was preferable to illiteracy for some of them.

For the freed slaves, literacy was at the top of their post-slavery list of tasks.[21] The fact that literacy would be of little practical use for freed slaves was irrelevant. After the Civil War, even the elderly desired to learn how to read prior to death. Myers says:

> Many of the older [Africans] wanted to learn to read the **Bible** before they died. In 1865, Richard Dennet, a northern correspondent, saw an old white-haired man among the children in a freedman's school in Mobile, Alabama. When asked why he was there, the old man responded, "I will not trouble the teacher much, but I must learn to read the **Bible** and the **Testament**." Tottering old men and women sat side by side with their

---

[20] ibid., 65-66.

[21] John B. Myers, "The Education of Alabama Freedmen During Presidential Reconstruction: 1865-1877," *Journal of Negro Education* 40 (Spring 1971):163.

children and grandchildren endeavoring to learn their letters.[22]

1.5 The Role of the African Preacher in the Interpretation of Biblical Texts

It is impossible to speak of the linkage between literacy, the **Bible**, and freedom, without speaking of the African preacher. It was through the preacher's proclamation of the **Bible's** message to the slave community that allowed the slaves to "make the Gospel their own." The late CME Bishop Joseph A. Johnson stated:

> Moving across the pages of history almost unnoticed by historians, [the African preacher] is one of the most colorful and dynamic figures ever to illuminate American folklore. Armed only with the grace of God and unique qualities of the gifts of [Africaness], this spiritual giant developed and preached the Gospel which enabled the [African] masses to transcend the vicissitudes of life....Man of God by calling—but often teacher, healer, caretaker, and undertaker by necessity, it was the [African] preacher who took down the

---

[22] ibid., 163-164.

mutilated bodies of [African] men after the mobs had done their worst.²³

By implication, Bishop Johnson informs us that the most feared, as well as respected figures in the American experience is the African preacher. The African preacher has traditionally led his community in resisting the destructive power of American society. He led the resistance by his ability to *interpret* the Word of God in such a way so as to contradict the de-Humanizing actions of American society.

Resistance could come in one of two forms. First, there was the possibility of open revolt. African preachers led three of the most famous, though failed, slave revolts in the early 1800s. These preachers *interpreted* the **Old Testament** in such a way as to lead their followers to believe that God condemned their oppression as well as their oppressors. Those preachers were, Richmond, Virginia's Gabriel Prosser, (1802), Charleston, South Carolina's Denmark Vesey, (1822), and South Hampton, Virginia's Nat Turner, (1831).²⁴

---

²³Bishop Joseph A. Johnson, Jr., *Proclamation Theology* (Shreveport, LA: Fourth Episcopal District Press, 1977), 39-40.

²⁴ Gayraud Wilmore, *Black Religion and Black Radicalism: An Interpretation of the Religious History of Afro-American People* (Maryknoll, NY, 1991), 53-73. Also, see Herbert Aptheker, American Negro Slave Revolts, 5th Edition New York: International Publishers, 1987). Revelations have surfaced over the last two decades that suggest the United States Government sees the African preacher as a force to be feared and reckoned with. Since the First World War, African preachers deemed to be radical subversives or threats to national security have been placed under

Another method of resistance was to quietly contradict the racist *interpretation* of the **Bible** during secret worship services. The late Howard Thurman remembers,

> When I was a youngster, my grandmother drilled this [idea] into me. The idea was given to her by a certain slave minister who, on occasions held secret religious meetings with his fellow slaves. How everything in me quivered with a pulsing tremor of raw energy when in her recital, she would come to the triumphal climax of the minister: "you—you are *not* niggers. You—you are *not* slaves, you are *God's children.*[Italics Added] [25]

---

surveillance and harassed by the Federal Government. The denomination they represented was irrelevant. Federal agents, *agent provocateurs*, and informants monitored Baptist and Pentecostals. Ironically, their views on America's participation in the Great War were irrelevant. Bishop C.H. Mason, organizer of the Church of God in Christ, condemned America's participation in "the War to Make the *World* Safe for Democracy," because Africans were not *safe* in America. Because of Bishop Mason's stand against the War, he was placed under observation. Robert M. Franklin, *Another Day's Journey: Black Churches Confront the American Crisis* (Minneapolis: Augsburg/Fortress Press, 1997), 50. Although the National Baptist Convention enthusiastically supported the War, its leadership was placed under surveillance. *The Commercial Appeal* (Memphis, TN), 31 March 1993.

[25] Howard Thurman, *Jesus and the Disinherited* (Nashville: Abingdon Press, 1949), 51.

1.6 The Present Day Situation of Africans in America

Recent events would suggest that African existence in America is still a questionable proposition. Africans are regarded as being less than Human, hence less than full participants in the American experience. An excellent illustration of this point is the infamous Tuskegee Study conducted by the United States Department of Public Health on unsuspecting African males in Alabama from the early 1930s until it was exposed in 1972.[26]

African Humanity is still a questionable proposition. The late William Schockley, a Nobel Prize winner and Stanford University professor, forwarded the ridiculous idea in a paper presented to the National Association for the Sciences in 1971 that the more white genes a person possessed, the more intelligent he was.[27] Two self-

---

[26] In the "study," African men, infected with syphilis, were never told of their condition. Instead their condition was allowed to go untreated for nearly forty years, while the effects of the disease were "studied." They were only told that they had "bad blood." James H. Jones, *Bad Blood: The Tuskegee Syphilis Experiment* (New York: The Free Press, 1993), ix-x, 1. This revelation has caused many observers to believe that the AIDS virus was developed by the government to eradicate African peoples, ibid. Also, Haki R. Madhubuti, *Black Men Obsolete, Single, Dangerous?: Afrikan-American Families in Transition: Essays in Discovery, Solution and Hope* (Chicago: Third World Press, 1991), 51-57.

[27] William Schockley, "Hardy-Weinberg Law Generalized to Estimate Hybrid Variance for Negro Populations and Reduce Racial Aspects of Environment-Hereditary Uncertainty," in Roger Pearson, ed., *Schockley on Eugenics: The Application of Science to the Solution of Human Problems* (Washington DC: Scott-Townsend Publishers, 1992), 170-171.

professed admirers of Schockley,[28] Richard J. Herrenstein and Charles Murray predicted that those with less intelligence, (Africans) will eventually be separated from the general population. They will become wards of what they call "the custodial state." Signs of the arrival of "the custodial state," are:

- Inner-city day care centers, homeless shelters, and public housing will be concentrated in specific areas.
- Strict policing and custodial responses to crime will become more acceptable and widespread.
- Racism will reemerge in a new and more dangerous form. [29]

What is this "custodial state"? Herrenstein and Murray reply:

> In short, by custodial state, we have in mind a high-tech and more lavish version of the Indian Reservation for some substantial minority of the nation's population, while

---

[28] Schockley's eccentric beliefs sparked controversy. He was so dedicated to the idea of the elimination of persons (primarily those of African descent) he deemed to have low intelligence, he proposed paying people with low IQs to be sterilized. He supported, as well as *contributed* to, a sperm bank for geniuses. Richard J. Herrnstein and Charles Murray, *The Bell Curve: Intelligence and Class Structure in American Life* (New York: The Free Press, 1994), 10.

[29] ibid., 525-526

the rest of America tries to go on about its business.[30]

The move towards what Herrenstein and Murray call a "high-tech version of the Indian Reservation" can be seen in the overwhelming numbers of African males involved in America's Criminal "Justice" system.

Just as recently as 1997, the National Baptist Convention, USA, Incorporated's Criminal Justice Commission reported:

> As of December 31, 1994, African-American men comprised nearly 44% (215, 400) of the nation's jail population and nearly 50% (456,570) of the nation's prison population. When you consider parole, probation, and those convicted awaiting to be incarcerated, over one million African...men are impacted by the justice system.[31]

African males that run afoul of the Criminal "Justice" system are profitable commodities. There are definite economic benefits to be realized by increasing the African

---

[30] ibid.

[31] National Baptist Convention, USA, Inc., Prison and Criminal Justice Commission, *Crime Prevention and Prison Ministry Program: Goals and Objectives* (St. Petersburg, FL: The National Baptist Convention, USA, Inc, 1997), 7.

male jail and prison population. After all, there is money to be made and jobs to be created with the construction of additional jails and prisons! There are support services that go along with imprisonment, i.e., uniforms for prisoners and guards, janitorial supplies, food for the inmates and staff. Concrete, barbed wire, electronic surveillance systems, tear gas, firearms, and pepper spray must be purchased. Imprisonment is more than locking a person up. It is a very profitable enterprise. Jerome G. Miller calls this process, "the Cold War of the 1990s."[32]

1.7 The Roots of the Problem

The basic problem of "Race" has never been lost on observant social commentators. W.E.B. DuBois wrote these famous words nearly four decades after the Civil War:

---

[32] This "Cold War" of the 1990s has its own version of the Military-Industrial Complex. Miller calls it the "Crime Control-Industrial Complex." With the collapse of Communism, a need arose to continue expenditures that had formerly been directed against the Soviet Union. The Cold War had produced jobs and profits for defense contractors. It was a simple matter then for some of those same contractors to seek conversion of their technologies to domestic use. With their resources now directed towards a domestic market, the target population became, instead of Russians, African Americans, specifically males. The new idea was to warehouse them in high-tech prisons. There is now a great demand for prisons to be built in rural areas. This is due to the economic boom caused by prison construction as well as vending opportunities. This assists the local population economically as well as the contractors that profit by warehousing African Men in prison. Jerome G. Miller, *Search and Destroy: African-American Males in the Criminal Justice System* (Cambridge, UK: Cambridge University Press, 1996), 228, 230-231.

> The problem of the Twentieth Century is the problem of the color line—the relation of the darker to the lighter races of men in Asia, Africa, and the islands of the Sea. It was a phase of the problem that caused the Civil War; and however much they who marched south and north in 1861 may have fixed on the technical points of union [versus] local autonomy as [an excuse], all nevertheless knew...that the question of [African] slavery was the real cause of the conflict. [33]

In the 1940s, Swedish sociologist, Gunnar Myrdal wrote:

> To the great majority of White Americans, the [African] problem has distinctively negative connotations. It is something difficult to settle and equally difficult to leave alone. It is embarrassing, it makes for moral uneasiness, The very presence of the [African] in America, his fate in this country through slavery, civil war, and Reconstruction, his recent career, and his present status, his accommodating, his protest and his aspirations, in fact his entire social existence as a participant American represent to the ordinary white man in the north as well as in the south an anomaly in the very structure of American society. To many, this takes on the proportion of a

---

[33] W.E.B. DuBois "The Souls of Black Folk" in *DuBois: Writings*, Nathan Huggins, ed. (New York: Library Classics, 1984), 372.

menace—biological, economic, social, cultural, and at times political. This anxiety may be mixed with a feeling of individual or collective guilt. A few see the problem as a challenge to statesmanship, *to all, it is trouble*. [Italics Added].[34]

Recent commentators such as Kenneth Clark[35] and Cornel West have failed to see much change.[36]

1.8 Chapter Summary

The basis of this chapter rests upon five points. First, **Biblical** texts have no meaning until they are *interpreted*. Second, persons of African descent have suffered throughout history because of the *misinterpretation* of **Biblical** texts, particularly the so-called "Curse of Ham." Third, persons of African descent have been able to rise above their suffering by *interpreting* the text for themselves. Fourth, relevant understandings of the text have always spoken to persons of African descent. Africans must *interpret* the **Bible** in the light of their experience so as to allow the Word of God to speak to their present circumstance. The alternative is to passively allow the

---

[34] Gunnar Myrdal, *An American Dilemma: The Negro Problem and Modern Democracy* (New York: Harper & Row, 1944), lxix.

[35] Kenneth Clark, "The Present Dilemma of the Negro," *Journal of Negro History* 53 (January 1968): 1.

[36] Cornel West, *Race Matters* (New York: Vintage Books, 1994), 4-7, 22-25.

nightmare of Herrenstein's and Murray's "Custodial State," to become a reality. Fifth, the events suggested in **Genesis** and in the Egyptian/**Exodus** experience are of great importance to both Africans as well as non-Africans. If this is so, we should *revisit* the **Book of Genesis**. As we revisit **Genesis** and find out what it *says* to persons of African descent in the waning hours of the Twentieth Century, perhaps we can face the uncertainty of the Twenty-First Century. For this cause the title of this book is, *From Eden to Egypt: The Book of Genesis Revisited.*

1.9 Suggestions for Further Reading

Anderson, Claud. *Black Labor, White Wealth: The Search For Power and Economic Justice.* Edgewood, MD: Duncan and Duncan Publishers, 1994.

Curtin, Phillip D. *The Atlantic Slave Trade: A Census.* Madison, WI: The University of Wisconsin Press, 1969.

Fitts, Leroy. *A History of Black Baptists.* Nashville: Broadman Press, 1985.

Franklin, John Hope. *From Slavery to Freedom: A History Of Negro Americans.* New York: Alfred A. Knopf, 1974.

Hamilton, Charles V. *The Black Preacher in America.* New York: William Morrow & Company, 1972.

Hitler, Adolf. *Mien Kampf.* New York: Stackploe Sons, 1939.

Jordan, Jr. Ervin. *Black Confederates and Afro-Yankees in Civil War Virginia.* Charlottesville, VA: The University of Virginia Press, 1995.

Lakey, Othal Hawthorne. *The History of the CME Church.* Memphis: The CME Publishing House, 1985.

McCoy, Alfred W. *The Politics of Heroin: CIA Complicity In the Global Drug Trade*. Brooklyn, NY: Lawrence Hill Books, 1991.

Ogbonnaya, A. Okechukwu. *Upon This Rock: African Influence in the Christian Church*. Chicago: Urban Ministries, Inc., 1999.

O'Reilly, Kenneth. *Black Americans and the FBI Files*. New York: Carroll & Graf, 1994.

Gentry, Curt. *J. Edgar Hoover: The Man and His Secrets*. New York: W.W. Norton, 1991.

Paris, Peter J. *Black Religious Leaders: Conflict in Unity*. Louisville, KY: Westminster/John Knox Press, 1991.

Popovic, Alexandre. *The Revolt of the African Slaves in Iraq in the $3^{rd}/9^{th}$ Century*. Translated by Leon King Princeton, NJ: Markus Wiener Publishers, 1999.

Shannon, David T. and Gayraud Wilmore. *Black Witness to The Apostolic Faith*. New York: The National Council Of Churches of Christ, 1985.

Walker, David. *Appeal To The Coloured Citizens Of The World, But In Particular, And Very Expressly, To Those Of The United States Of America*, ed., Charles M. Wiltse. New York: Hill and Wang, 1965.

Washington, Linn. *Black Judges on Justice*. New York: The Free Press, 1995.

Watts, Deborah A. *101 Ways to Know You're "Black" in Corporate America*. Plymouth, MN: Watts-Five Productions, 1998.

Webb, Gary. *Dark Alliance: The CIA, the Contras, and the Crack Cocaine Explosion*. New York: Seven Stories Press, 1998.

Wilmore, Gayraud. *Black Religion and Black Radicalism: An Interpretation of the Religious History of Afro-American People*. Maryknoll, NY: Orbis Press, 1991.

_____, ed. *Black Men in Prison: The Response of the African-American Church*. Atlanta: The ITC Press, 1990.

Wright, Bruce. *Black Robes, White Justice: Why Our Legal System Doesn't Work for Blacks*. New York: The Carol Publishing Group, 1994.

57

"... How can [our] enemies... say that we and our children are not of the Human family. But were made by our Creator to be an inheritance to them and theirs forever?"

David Walker (1785-1830), African Christian and Abolitionist
Died under mysterious circumstances in Boston, Massachusetts

"God made the world as well as everything that exists...The entire Human Race descended from one person...God determines the history of every nation and where they should live." Acts 17:24-26

The Apostle Paul, c. 40 AD

Chapter 2

The Book of Genesis: Its Place in the Old Testament and its Relationship to Human Origins

2.1 Chapter Introduction

Chapter 2 proposes two objectives. First, we will look at the word "**Genesis,**" and show how this book got its name. Second, we will look at Africa and Human origins from three standpoints: **Biblical**, scientific, and that of "floating" African traditions.

2.2 The Book of Genesis: the Origin of its Name

The title "**Genesis**" is not the original name for the first book in the **Bible**. The title "**Genesis**" is derived from the name assigned by the Second Century BC translators of the **Old Testament,** as well as Jewish writings that are not considered "inspired," into Greek. That translation is known as the *Septuagint*. [1]

---

[1] The Septuagint's origins are shrouded in legend. It derives its name from the number "Seventy." It is often referred to in writing as the **LXX** (the Roman numeral for 70). Legend has it that Pharaoh Ptolemy Philadelphus of Egypt (285-246 BC), requested that the Jewish High Priest, Eleazar, dispatch six scholars from each of the Twelve Tribes of Israel from Judah to Egypt. The request was granted and seventy-two scholars went to Egypt. According to the legend, each had a small room in which to work. The legend goes on to state that within a seventy-two day period, each scholar produced an identical and accurate copy of the Jewish **SCRIPTURES**. Charles F. Pfeiffer, *Between the Testaments* (Grand Rapids, MI: Baker Book House, 1959), 85. The **Book of Genesis** is the first book in the *Pentateuch*. The word "Pentateuch" is derived from two Greek words, *pente*=five and

The title **Genesis** is derived from the first words in **Genesis 2:4a**, as found in the *Septuagint*, "This is the book of the origins, (*geneseos*) of the heavens and the earth."[2] Jewish tradition named this book, *Beresit*, or "In the beginning." The Hebrew word *Beresit*, in contrast to the word *geneseos*, derives, in part, from the very first words of the book itself, "In the beginning..." (**Genesis 1:1**).[3] The **Book of Genesis** is not a science text, but it deals with the *geneseos* or *origins* of the world and Humankind. In order to understand the *geneseos*, we must begin in Africa. In fact, the focus of this study begins in an African garden named Eden and ends in an African nation named Egypt.

2.3 Africa and Human Origins: Textual Evidence

The first step toward *reinterpreting* the **Book of Genesis** for our day is to look at its African context. Humankind, according to **Genesis 2:4-14**, arises out of Eden. And Eden, as we will suggest, arises out of Africa.

The following passage in **Genesis 2:4-14** suggests a key to our understanding of Africa and its relationship with Human origins.

---

teuchos=tool. The other "tools," are **Exodus, Leviticus, Numbers**, and **Deuteronomy**. Claus Westermann, *Handbook of the Old Testament*, trans. Robert H. Boyd (Minneapolis: Augsburg Press, 1967), 13.

[2] Ronald S. Hendel, "Book of Genesis," in the *Anchor Bible Commentary*.

[3] ibid.

A summary of **Genesis 2:4-14** could go as follows:

- In **2:4-6**, there is no animal or plant life. There were only subterranean streams that spew forth water, which in turn drench the earth.

- In verse **7**, a man was created (in Hebrew *Adam* translates to our English word, "man"). God animated him by breathing into his nostrils, the "breath of life."

- In verses **9-10**, God planted a garden, "in the East." God placed Adam in the Garden to tend it.

- The phrase "in the East," in verse **8**, does not tell us much. However, in verses **10-11**, the writer gets specific. He tells us that there is a river that springs from the garden. The river then divides itself into four headwaters. The first river, Pishon winds through Havilah. The second river, Gihon, winds through the land of Cush. The third river, the Tigris, runs by the land of Asshur. The fourth river is identified as being the Euphrates.

By the location of the first two rivers, Pishon and Gihon, it could be argued that the Garden of Eden was located in Africa. After all, the Hebrew name, *Cham* (transliterated into English as *Ham*), means "burnt" or "Black," Ham of course was one of the sons of Noah, (**Genesis 6:10** and **10:18**). Ham was the father of Cush, (**Genesis 10:6**), whose name in Hebrew also means "burnt" or "Black." Among Cush's sons, we find Havilah (**Genesis 10:6**. According to **Genesis 2:11,** the Land of Havilah borders one of Eden's rivers, the Pishon. The Pishon flows from the Garden of Eden). The land of Cush was located in the area of modern day Sudan, in East Africa. This region has always been associated with Black-skinned peoples, in fact the word, *Sudan* is derived from an Arabic word meaning "Black" or "burnt." Adamo, basing his findings upon Egyptian, Greek, and Assyrian sources, argues persuasively, that the Gihon refers to the Nile River.[4]

2.4 Africa and Human Origins: Scientific Evidence

The late African anthropologist Cheikh Anta Diop, basing his findings upon the pioneering work of Louis Leakey, placed the origin of the Human Race in East Africa. In fact, Humanity as we know it today, according to Diop, originated in the Great Lakes region around the Omo Valley 150,000 years ago.[5]

---

[4]David Tuesday Adamo, "Ancient Africa and Genesis 2:10-14," *Journal of Religious Thought* 49:1 (Summer-Fall, 1992): 38-40.

[5]Diop, *Civilization or Barbarism*, 11. The late Louis B. Leakey was born in what is now Kenya, East Africa. He spent the better part of his life doing research on Human origins. Leakey is most famous for his excavations of East Africa's Olduvai Gorge. Through painstakingly slow efforts, Leakey and his wife Mary found Human remains, as well as tools dating back at least 1,700,000 years. John Pfeiffer, *The Emergence of Man* (New York: Harper & Row Publishers, 1969), 74-75. Recent fossil discoveries in Ethiopia suggest an even earlier origin of Humankind. The so-called "Lucy," discovery in Ethiopia pushes Human origins back at least 3,400,000 years, *San Francisco Chronicle* (San Francisco*)*, 18 November 1993.

If this is the case, two suggestions can be offered. First, it would seem the Human Race originated around the Earth's Equator. The Equator is hot and humid. Diop argues, according to Gloger's Law, that the original Humans had to be *Black-skinned*.[6] Secondly, if the oldest traces of what we understand to be Humanity originated in Africa, then it stands to reason that *all* races arise from the first Humans. These Humans were *Black*.[7]

Other discoveries suggest the Human Race originated in Africa. In 1984, an American Space Shuttle's instruments picked up what appeared to be the remains of an ancient river system in the southern portion of Egypt. With its powerful instruments, it was able to see from space what could not be seen by the naked eye on the ground. This ancient river system, complete with a valley, channel,

---

[6]Diop says, "[h]umankind, born around the Great Lakes region [of East Africa], almost on the Equator, is necessarily pigmented and *Black*; ...Gloger's Law calls for warm blooded animals [mammals] to be pigmented in a hot and humid climate." Diop, *Civilization or Barbarism*, 11. Finch puts it simply, "...the closer an animal is to the equator, the darker his coat. The polar bear, the arctic fox, and the snowshoe rabbit are all examples of winterized white coated Arctic animals that illustrate Golger's Law." Finch, *Echoes of the Old Darkland*, 36.

[7]Diop goes on to say, "...[a]ll other races derive from the Black race by more or less filtration, and the other continents were populated from Africa at the *Homo erectus* and *Homo sapien* stages, 150,000 years ago. The old theories that used to state that Blacks came from somewhere else are now invalid." Diop, *Civilization or Barbarism*, 11. Diop's suggestion would render Rabbinical interpretation of **Genesis 9:18-27**, as being an explanation for Black physical "characteristics," ridiculous.

and sandbar, is completely covered with a layer of sand. The river system's complexity and size rivals that of the Nile.[8]

Subsequent investigation by the Geological Survey of Egypt, the United States Agency for International Development, and the United States Geological Survey found evidence of tools and other signs of Human presence at the site. Similar artifacts have been found in Europe. The space shuttle's discovery caused researchers to suggest that Black Africans migrated to Europe. The Africans may have done so by following this river system.[9] If Adamo's suggestion is correct that the Gihon River is the Nile, then there is a strong possibility that the Pishon River, named in **2:11** could be part of the river system found in 1984.

2.5 Genesis and Human Origins: Evidence From "Generalized" African Traditions

The last piece of evidence pointing to Africa as the location of Eden is what I call "generalized" African traditions. These traditions are "generalized," because they are held in common by many of the Black-skinned inhabitants of Africa.

These traditions relate to the creation and "fall" of Humankind. They can be called "generalized," because in "particular" instances, they differ from group to group. An

---

[8] Adamo, "Ancient Africa and Genesis", 42.

[9] ibid.

interesting aspect of these traditions is that they bear strong resemblance to portions of **Genesis**. John S. Mbiti, a Kenyan clergyman and scholar, provides the following summary of many of these African belief systems.

> Whatever the story may be, the ideas are that: (i) man was created by God; (ii) in almost every case it was either husband and wife, or two pairs; (iii) the creation of man generally took place at the end of other things. This last point may indicate that people believe that man was the completion or perfection of God's work of creation, since nothing else better than man was created afterwards. [10]

By using Mbiti's suggestions, we can see possible connections between African religious beliefs and certain aspects of the **Genesis** accounts of Eden, and the creation of the Human Race. Observe:

- Man was created by God =**2:7**
- The husband and wife =**2:18**
- The creation of Human Beings comes last =**2:7**

He also notes the tradition of the "Tree of Life," as found as far south as Namibia.[11] This could suggest a

---

[10] John S. Mbiti, *Introduction to African Religion*, 2d ed.Oxford, UK: Heinemann Educational Publishers, 1975), 84.

[11] ibid., 86.

linkage between African traditions and the **Biblical** account of the "Tree of the Knowledge of Good and Evil," as found in **2:17**.

In many African belief systems, the intimate relationship between God and Humans was severed.[12] Though the reasons differ from place to place, African traditions suggest, at one time, the relationship between God and Humankind was harmonious. Compare this with **Genesis 2:15-25**. This relationship was disrupted due to Humans breaking God's commandments (**Genesis 3:1-23**). As a result, death and disease entered the world.[13]

Adamo calls the belief systems, "floating traditions," because they circulated in oral form throughout Africa and were probably passed along from generation to generation since time immemorial.[14]

Since Egypt's earliest inhabitants were Black-skinned Africans,[15] and these Black-skinned persons ruled that land during the time of Israel's residency in that country, it stands to reason that the Israelites may have come into contact with such stories of Eden, creation, and the fall

---

[12]ibid.

[13]ibid.

[14]Adamo, "Ancient Africa and Genesis," 36.

[15]Diop suggests that Black-skinned Africans first settled the Nile Valley 15,000-20,000 years ago. Diop, *Civilization or Barbarism*, 17.

from the Black Egyptians. Adamo also suggests that since Egypt is an African country, and that **Biblical** Egypt was certainly Black, these traditions could have found their way into the Hebrew concepts found in **Genesis 2-3**.

Adamo suggests that the traditions were absorbed by the Israelites in three ways, two of which are relevant to our discussion. First, since the **Bible** states that the Israelites stayed in Egypt for 430 years, (**Exodus 12:40**), they would have had to come into contact with African creation stories. The Cushite population, which formed the bulk of the army and police force, was quite large in Egypt at that time. The Israelites could have come into contact with the stories by way of these Cushites.[15] This theory should be taken seriously. As the author of the **Acts of the Apostles** relates, Moses, Israel's leader during the **Exodus** and Wilderness Periods, was "educated in *all* of the wisdom of the Egyptians..." (**Acts 7:22**). This could have very well been one of the ways Israel absorbed the "floating tradition" of the Creation, Eden, and the Fall of Humankind.

2.6 Chapter Summarization

An introduction to the **Book of Genesis** and Human origins must take into account the special relationship

---

[15]The second possibility is the Israelites heard about these traditions via the Mesopotamians, whom in turn received them from the Egyptians through their extensive trade and cultural ties. According to Adamo, these ties go back at least 3000 years before the birth of Christ. Adamo, "Ancient Africa and Genesis," 36. According to the Table of Nations, Mesopotamia was settled by Cushites (**Genesis 10:8-11**).

between the Continent of Africa and the appearance of the first Human Beings.

We have confronted this relationship on three fronts. First, we suggested that fossil data, specifically in East Africa's Omo Valley, along with the effects of Gloger's Law upon mammals, points to the earliest remains of our common ancestors. Second, a combination of **Biblical** and scientific findings point to the location of the Garden of Eden as East Africa. This was done by relating the names and locations of the first two rivers that spring from Eden, Gihon and Pishon, **(2:11-12)**, to the Nile and another river system discovered by an American Space Shuttle in 1984. Third, creation stories bearing a strong resemblance to those found in **Genesis 2:5-26** and **3**, or "floating traditions," abound throughout Africa. These stories transcend culture and historical settings. The suggestion at this point is these traditions are rooted in the memories of the African descendants of the world's first Human Beings, i.e., Black-skinned *Africans*. These traditions then "floated" into the beliefs and faith of Israel.

We began our examination of **Genesis** in Eden; let us move on.

2.7 Suggestions For Further Reading

Anyike, James C. *Historical Christianity African Centered Proving the Vital Role of Black People in Establishing Early Christianity, Dispelling the Myth that Christianity Is the White Man's Religion.* Chicago: Popular Truth, Inc., 1995.

Adamo, David Tuesday. "Ancient Africa and **Genesis** 2:10-14," *Journal of Religious Thought* 49:1 (September-Fall 1992): 33-43.

_____. *Africa and the Africans in the Old Testament.* Bethesda, MD: The Christian Universities Press, 1998.

Diop, Cheikh Anta. *Civilization or Barbarism: An Authentic Anthropology*, trans. Yaa-Lengi Meema Ngemi. Brooklyn, NY: Lawrence Hill Books, 1991.

_____. *The African Origin of Civilization: Myth or Reality*, Translated by, Mercer Cook. Brooklyn, NY: Lawrence Hill Books, 1974.

_____. *The Cultural Unity of Negro Africa: The Domains of Patriarchy and Matriarchy in Classical Antiquity.* Paris: Pre'sence Africaine, 1962.

Finch III, Charles S. *Echoes of the Old Darkland: Themes From the African Eden.* Khenti, Inc., 1992.

Poe, Richard. *Black Spark, White Fire: Did African Explorers Civilize Ancient Europe?* Rocklin, CA: Prima Publishing, 1997.

Stringer, Christopher and Robin McKie. *African **Exodus**: The Origins of Modern Humanity.* New York: Henry Holt and Company, 1997.

"By virtue of the power and for the purpose aforesaid, I do order and declare that all persons held as slaves within said designated [Southern rebel] States and parts of States are, and henceforward shall be, free; and that the Executive Government of the United States, including the military and naval authorities thereof, will recognize and maintain the freedom of said persons.

And I hereby enjoin upon the people so declared to be free to abstain from all violence, unless in necessary self-defense; and I recommend to them that, in all cases when allowed, they labor faithfully for reasonable wages."

The Emancipation Proclamation, 1863
President Abraham Lincoln

Chapter 3

Ham, His Descendants and Ancient Civilization

3.1 Chapter Introduction

In **Chapter 1**, we saw how Jewish, Muslim and Christian *interpretations* of **Genesis 9:18-27** distorted an angry outburst by a "hung over" Noah. This resulted in awful stereotypes and the *de*-Humanization of African peoples in the eyes of non-Africans. In **Chapter 2**, the special relationship between Africa and the creation narratives of **Genesis 2:4-24, 3** in light of Human origins was explored. Three levels of evidence, scientific, **Biblical**, and "floating African traditions," provided strong indications that Africa, specifically the Omo Valley in the eastern part of the continent, provided the earliest examples of present day Humanity. We looked at the research findings of Diop, who in turn based his conclusions on the strength of Gloger's Law, and Leakey's research indicates Humanity had its beginnings in that area. Second, **Genesis 2:10-13,** suggests that the Garden of Eden was located in Eastern Africa. The two rivers mentioned in that passage of **Scripture**, Gihon and Pishon, are in all probability the River Nile and a recently discovered river system in Eastern Africa. Third, African traditions surrounding Human origins strongly suggest that they influenced the creation stories in **Genesis**.

Africa, in the popular mind, is viewed as a place of savagery. It was called the "Dark Continent," by the European exploiters at an early stage of their involvement with Africa. From the 1600s to the present, Africa served as an inexhaustible pool of cheap labor and source for raw materials. After the slave trade ended, around the mid-1800s, the Europeans carved up the continent amongst themselves. The turning point for this unfortunate state of affairs was the infamous Conference of Berlin (1885) hosted by Kaiser Wilhelm II, the German Emperor. At the conference, the European powers divided the continent amongst themselves into colonies. The "Curse of Ham," no doubt played its part in this awful chain of events. After all, the African was "cursed" and a "savage" to boot. It was really to the African's "advantage" that the Europeans bring them the "light" of civilization, even if it did cost them their freedom. The rationale for bringing the "light" of civilization to the Black "heathens" of Africa, as well as to other non-whites, was provided by such European supporters of white superiority as the British poet and advocate for European and American colonialism, Rudyard Kipling (1865-1936). Perhaps his poem, *The White Man's Burden*,[1] best typified the age.

Were the Africans "savages"? Based upon the so-called "curse" placed on Ham by his father Noah, were they less than Human? In this chapter, the following question will be explored. What was the role of Ham and his descendants in the construction of civilization? In order

---

[1] For the full text of *The White Man's Burden*, see **Appendix B** on Page 149.

to do this, we will briefly look at the relationship of the founding head of a family and his relationship to his descendants and the land that the family settled. We will also take a close look at the general role played by Ham and his children in the construction of what we now call "civilization." Then we will look at the far-flung influence of Ham's children upon places far removed from his African home. Also, just as we used **Biblical** as well as non-**Biblical** sources in **Chapter 2** to explore **Genesis'** relationship to Human origins, the same will be done to explore the influence of Ham and his family upon what we call, "civilization."

3.2 The Relationship of the Family Head, His Descendants, and Land Occupation

Biblically speaking, the founding member of a family settled territory. The founder was forever linked to that land by way of his family's occupancy of the land. In fact, sometimes, God would speak to the inhabitants of the land in a manner that suggested He was still speaking directly to the founding head of the family. God would speak in this manner even if that person had died centuries before (**Isaiah 40:27**). Also, the **Biblical** writers would often refer to a nation as if the founder were still alive. This was because the geographical area occupied by the founder's descendants was generally called the land of, "Canaan," "Israel," "Judah," "Egypt," etc.

3.3 Ham, His Descendants [1] and Their Civilizing Influence

The presence and prominence of Ham's family presupposes The Great Flood (**Genesis 6-8**) that destroyed the inhabited world. God caused the flood. He sought to make a new beginning after the Human Race, according to **Genesis 6:5-7**, became thoroughly corrupt.

After the Flood, Ham's family made its presence felt throughout the ancient world. They roamed far and wide and settled vast tracts of land. As they settled, they founded great cities and civilizations. Ham's descendants are named in the Table of Nations (**Genesis 10:6-20**). The graph on pages **Pages 11** and **78** gives a pictorial representation of this so-called "**Table.**"

The English transliteration of the Hebrew word *Cham* is "Ham." *Cham* means "burnt'" or "Black." The same goes for the Hebrew word, "*Cush*," it also means "burnt'" or "Black." It stands to reason then if "Ham" and "Cush" translate to "burnt" or "Black," then their descendents were—"***BLACK.***"

It is a common misconception to confine Black-skinned people to the continent of Africa. A further misconception places them in other locales only due to modern population movements such as the European slave trade that literally transplanted millions of Africans to the so-called "New World." This could not be farther from the

---

[1] For a visualization of Ham's family, see the graph on **Pages 11** and **78**.

truth. Ham's family traveled the globe during ancient times at their own volition. In their wake, they planted the seeds of modern civilization.[2]

3.4 Ham, His Descendents and Their Civilizing Influence

Scientific evidence strongly suggests Human Beings, as we know them, originated in the Omo Valley of East Africa. After the Great Flood of **Genesis 6**, according to **Genesis 10**, the world began to repopulate. A close look at **Genesis 10's TABLE OF NATIONS** reveals the settlement patterns of Noah's sons.

According to **Genesis 10:6-19**, the most important cities and civilizations of the ancient world were founded by Ham's descendants. Observe:

- Of Ham's four sons, Cush, Mizraim, and Canaan are of interest to us. Cush and Mizraim (**10:6**) are especially interesting because of their immediate relationship to Africa. Cush settled south of Egypt. And Mizraim, another name for Egypt, occupied the land in the northeastern corner of Africa. Canaan occupied the land

---

[2] Contrary to popular opinion, the original inhabitants of the world were Black-skinned people. There is at present, as **Chapter 2** indicates, an extensive body of research that suggests that the world's original inhabitants were Black. If, as the evidence suggests, the original inhabitants of the world were Black-skinned, would it not stand to reason that Adam, Eve, Cain, Abel, and even Noah *had Black skin*? And if Noah had *Black* skin, his curse upon Canaan, was an angry outburst fueled by alcohol, not, as the Rabbis, Muslims and European Christians suggests—Divine authority!

directly to the northeast of Egypt. This land was later allocated to Abraham and his family (**12:1-8**). Egypt (Mizraim) extended his settlements throughout the Mediterranean and, most interesting, to the Island of Crete. This island is identified in the text as the dwelling place of the Casluhhites ("from whom the Philistines came," **10:14**).

- Havilah, a son of Cush, (**10:7**) settled south of Egypt. The lands of Cush and Havilah are related to the rivers that flow from Eden (**2:10**).

- Cush was the father of Nimrod (**10:8**). Nimrod founded several cities in Mesopotamia. The most outstanding two cities were Babylon and Nineveh (**10:10-11**).

- One of Cush's sons was Canaan, who fathered the settlers of Sidon (later known as Lebanon or Phoenicia), the Hittites and the Jesbusites. The Jebusites founded and lent their name to a city, which bears their name to this day—Jerusalem (**10:15**).

The text of **Genesis** provides a framework for discussion concerning Ham's children and ancient civilization. In other words, it provides the springboard for our discussion of Ham's influence upon, not only the ancient world, but also what we call "civilization." Let us now proceed from that springboard.

The Table of Nations With Reference To Noah and Ham
Genesis 9:18, 10: 6-19

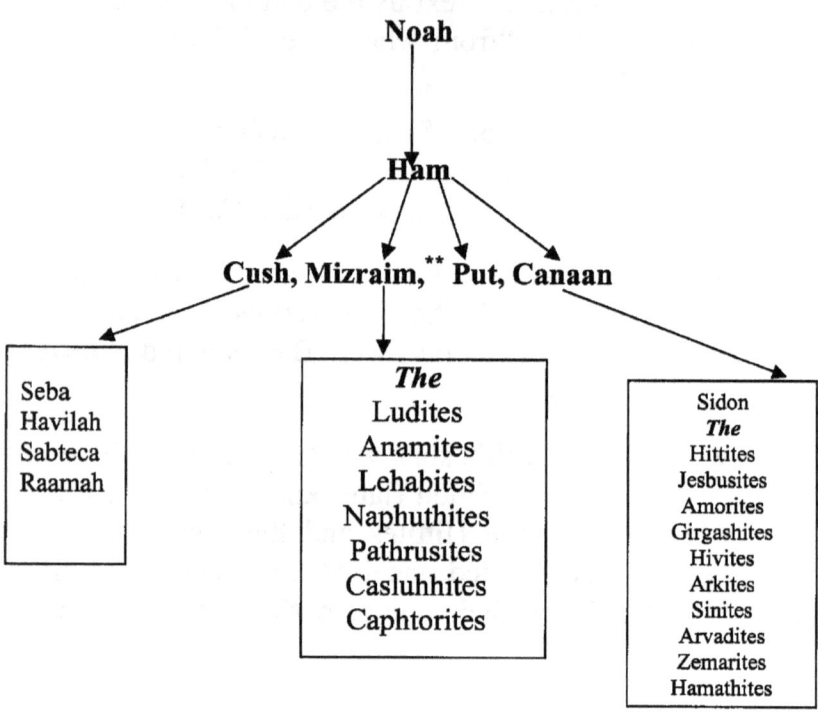

** **Mizaim** is also known as **Egypt**

3.5 The Egyptian/Cushite Role in the Process of Civilization

In *3.3*, we noted the relationship between the English transliteration of Noah's middle son's name, Ham and the Hebrew word "Cham", meaning "burnt" or "Black." The ancient Egyptians called their land *"Kemet."* Kemet is related to the word *Cham*. *Kemet* means, "Land of the *Blacks*." The English transliteration of the word Kemet is Egypt.[3]

Egypt is key to our understanding of the ancient world; it was arguably the world's first civilized state, with a history dating back at least 10,000 years, maybe even 39,000 years![4] The Black African presence in Northeastern Africa goes back at least 700,000 years! Egypt settled in Northeastern Africa, but unashamedly spread his influence throughout the ancient world. In modern terminology, Egypt was a "super power."

---

[3] Diop, *The African Origin of Civilization*, 7. Since Egypt (Mizraim) and his brother Cush had such a tremendous impact upon world progress and ancient civilization, so as to avoid confusion, whenever I speak of Egypt, I am also speaking of Cush. The Egyptians invented the device we know today as the calendar. They were the world's first astronomers. Astronomical projections are related to mathematical precision. This allowed the Egyptians to measure time not only in days, weeks, months, and years, but millennia (thousand year units). This allowed Egyptian astronomers to calculate the age of their civilization as being at least 39,000 years old. Finch, *Echoes of the Old Darkland*, 123.

[4] ibid.

Closely related to Egypt was his brother Cush. Cush settled in Africa south of Egypt. Since they shared such close geographical proximity, it is sometimes hard to distinguish between the two. However, their descendents laid the foundation for our modern civilization through their population movements and settlement patterns.

The descendants of these two energetic brothers swept across the ancient world in a farther swath than even the **Biblical** text suggests. According to Dillard,

> Cush, through his descendants ...established eminent empires throughout China, India Afghanistan, etc., **Biblically**, historically, and physically, many of the original Asians were a product of "Cush" who gradually settled in the East following the break up of Babel (**Genesis 11:8-9**).[5]

The original inhabitants of the Indus Valley region, modern day India, were Black-skinned.[6]

The original inhabitants of Asia, in general, but China in particular, were Blacks that were short in stature. These

---

[5] Dillard, ***Biblical*** *Ancestry Voyage*, 57.

[6] Excavations conducted in 1925 show the presence of an advanced Black civilization, dating back to at least 2500 BC. Hood, *Begrimed and Black,* 4. The remnants of India's African inhabitants are now in the southern part of that country. They are known as the Dravidians. Rogers, *Sex and Race*, 62-63.

Blacks are still found in the Philippine Islands, where they are known as *Negritos,* (Spanish for "Small Blacks"). These *Negritos,* number around 31,000. They are divided into approximately twenty-nine language groups. They live mostly along the eastern coast of the island of Luzon. They mainly reside in the island's rain forests. About one third of them speak a language called *Agta.*[7] These small Blacks are also found in Central Africa where they are known in the Western World as "Pygmies." These people *never* called themselves "Pygmies," they call themselves the "Twa." These short Africans, according to ancient Chinese records, were China's first inhabitants.[8]

Ham's children can also be found in the South Pacific. Islands such as Fiji and New Guinea contain populations of Black-skinned,[9] woolly haired persons that are virtually

---

[7] Thomas N. Headland and P. Bin Griffin, *A Bibliography of the Agta Negritos of Eastern Luzon,* Philippines (Dallas: SIL Electronic Working Papers 1997-004, June 1997), 1.

[8] Brunson passes on the following: "During the Tsin-Ch'in dynasty (280-420 AD), reference is made to "Black dwarfs," in the mountainous districts of Yangtze.... Between AD 772-846, specific reference is made to an ebony-hued people in Southern Hunan province. As late as this period, many areas south of the Yangtze River were still considered the "ends of the earth," where goblins and demons dwelled." James E. Brunson, *Black Jade: African Presence in the Ancient East and Other Essays* (Dekalb, Ill: Kara Publishing Company, 1985), 6. The descendents of these short Blacks are found living on islands off the coast of Indochina (Vietnam). They are virtually indistinguishable from African Blacks. Finch, *Echoes of the Old Darkland,* 38. Also see, Rogers, *Sex and Race,* 67-68.

[9] ibid., 72-77.

indistinguishable from Africans in the Americas or even Africa.

Not only did Ham's children go east into Asia, and the South Pacific, but also strong evidence suggests that the original inhabitants of Europe were African. Skeletons, identified as African, were first discovered in the Grimaldi Caves of Monaco in the southeastern region of France in 1901 by the French anthropologist Rene Verneau.[10] These skeletal remains indicate a more far flung African presence than previously imagined.

It could be argued that these "Grimaldi" men might have been descendants of Ham. These Hamites may have been those Africans that were thought to have migrated to Europe following the riverbed found by the American Space Shuttle in 1984.[11] Although exact dating is

---

[10] Since Verneau's discoveries, "Grimaldi" type skeletons have been found from Continental Europe's most Western reach, Spain, all the way to eastern Europe's Siberia. Diop, *Civilization or Barbarism*, 13-15. Clegg presents a persuasive case for a Pygmy/Twa presence in Northern Europe, Greenland, the Arctic Circle and the Northeastern Coast of North America, as late as 1000-AD 1632. They were called the *Skrellings*. The term derives from a Nordic word for "small, "wizened," or "shriveled." Eskimo legends also speak of the Skrellings as Black dwarfs that lived in subterranean dwellings. Legrand H. Clegg II, "The Mystery of the Arctic Twa: A Letter to the Editor," in *African Presence in Early Europe*, Ivan Van Sertima, ed.New Brunswick, NJ: Transaction Publishers, 1996), 244-249. It could be argued that the legends of elves, "wee-folk," and leprechauns that circulate throughout Europe, even to this day, reflect vague historical memories of its first settlers, Africans of short stature. Finch, *Echoes of the Old Darkland*, 33-34.

[11] Adamo, "Ancient Africa and Genesis," 42.

impossible, one would be hard pressed to deny Dillard's claim that:

> Cush and his sons possessed civilization for thousands of years, with great arts, sciences, and public works, while Asia and China were barbaric, and London and Paris were swamplands, and Athens and Rome were vacant sites. The Hamitic descendants through Cush and his sons...[gave the] world much of what we now enjoy.[12]

As mentioned earlier, Egyptian civilization had risen and flourished at least 39,000 years, or more, before the birth of Christ.[13] This period witnessed Egypt lay the foundation for the science and technology that we take for granted.[14]

Egypt and Cush influenced more than Africa, Europe and Asia. Professor Ivan Van Sertima, of Rutgers

---

[12] Dillard, *Black Ancestry Voyage*, 67-68.

[13] Finch, *Echoes of the Old Darkland*, 123

[14] Hilliard lists the following examples of scientific and technological innovations developed by the Black Egyptians. His list is inclusive of, but not limited to, mathematics, astronomy, the calendar (the great traveling historian/scholar—known to us as the "Father of History"—Herodotus credits the Egyptians with the invention of the calendar. For his comments, see **Appendix C on** Page 154), engineering and architecture. Asa G. Hilliard III, *The Maroon Within Us: Selected Essays on African-American Community Socialization* (Baltimore: Black Classics Press, 1995), 91.

University, suggests their technological innovations and advances in navigational arts allowed them to sail to the "New" World. Upon their arrival, they proceeded to influence such pre-Columbian cultures as the Olmecs of present day Mexico.[15]

3.6 Chapter Summarization

In a manner similar to that of Chapter 2, a combination of textual and non-textual evidences shows that the world is in Africa's debt. The Table of Nations (**Genesis 10**) shows two things. First, far from being a "cursed" people, Ham and his descendants spread far and wide. They did not settle as vagrants and squatters, but as civilizers and city builders. Second, non-**Biblical** evidence provides strong evidence of African presence scattered throughout the ancient world, from Europe to India to China, the South Pacific, and even to the Americas!

---

[15] Van Sertima argues that the Cushites, or Nubians as they were sometimes called, came into contact with the Olmec Indians of present day Mexico sometime between 948-680 BC. Whether they went there for the purpose of exploration and trade or were accidentally blown off course is not known. But it is apparent they may have stayed long enough to influence Olmec social development. Apparently the Egyptian/Cushite explorers had a tremendous impact on Olmec civilization. Their legacy can be seen in the massive stone heads, weighing several tons, with distinctly *African* features. Ivan Van Sertima, "Egyptio-Nubian Presence in Ancient Mexico," in *The African Presence in Early America* (New Brunswick. NJ: Transaction Publishers, 1992), 55-81. Also, Ivan Van Sertima, *They Came Before Columbus: The African Presence in Ancient America* (New York: Random House, 1976), 142-179.

If the world is in such debt to its common African ancestry, what happened to reverse this fabulous era of peace, prosperity and progress? How did non-Africans, specifically those who came to be known as "Europeans" position themselves to declare their "supremacy"? What caused this reverse in the fortunes of Ham's children? In order to suggest answers to these questions, we must now look at Egypt and its times of "troubles."

3.7 Suggestions For Further Reading

Bernal, Martin. "Black Athena: The African and Levantine Roots of Greece," in *African Presence in Europe*, Ivan Van Sertima, ed. New Brunswick, NJ: Transaction Publishers, 1996.

Brunson, James. "The African Presence in the Ancient Mediterranean Isles and Ancient Greece," in *The African Presence in Early Europe*, Ivan Van Sertima, ed. New Brunswick, NJ: Transaction Publishers, 1996.

Clegg II, LeGrand. "The Mystery of the Arctic Twa: A Letter to the Editor," in *African Presence in Early Europe*," Ivan Van Sertima, ed. New Brunswick, NJ: Transaction Publishers, 1996.

Dearman, J. Andrew. "The Family in the Old Testament," *Interpretation: A Journal of **Bible** and Theology* 52:2 (April 1998): 117-129.

Felder, Cain Hope, ed. *Stony The Road We Trod: African-American **Biblical** Interpretation.* Minneapolis: Augsburg/Fortress Press, 1991.

Luke, Don. "African Presence in the Early History of The British Isles and Scandinavia," in *The African Presence in Early Europe*, Ivan Van Sertima, ed. New Brunswick: NJ: Transaction Publishers, 1996.

Rashhidi, Runoko. *Introduction to the Study of Ancient African Civilizations*. Chicago: Karnack House, 1992.

_____. "Ancient and Modern Britons: An Essay," in *African Presence in Early Europe*. Ivan Van Sertima, ed. New Brunswick, NJ: Transaction Publishers, 1996.

Rogers, J.A. *Sex and Race: Negro-Caucasian Mixing in All Ages and in All Lands*, Vol. 1, *The Old World*. St. Petersburg, FL: Helga Rogers, 1967.

Van Sertima, Ivan and Rashidi Runoko, ed. *African Presence in Early Asia*. New Brunswick, NJ: Transaction Publishers, 1988.

Van Sertima, Ivan, ed. *African Presence in Early America*. New Brunswick, NJ: Transaction Publishers, 1992.

_____. *Egypt Revisited*. New Brunswick, NJ: Transaction Publishers, 1995.

_____. *They Came Before Columbus: The African Presence in America*. (New York: Random House, 1976.

"Give me liberty, or give me death"

Patrick Henry, American Revolutionary War Patriot

"The only tactical principle which is not subject to change; is this, ...to use the means at hand to inflict the maximum amount of wounds, death, and destruction on the enemy in the minimum amount of time. War is simple, direct, and ruthless."

George S. Patton
US Army General, World War II

Chapter 4

Egypt and Its "Time of Troubles"

4.1 Chapter Introduction

The Black African presence in the Nile Valley goes back at least 700,000 years. Egyptian society/civilization may go back 39,000 years or more before the birth of Christ.[1] Prior to 4000 BC, whites were absent from Egypt.[2] African civilization and stability was effected by the arrival of successive waves of foreign invasions, beginning around 3150-3000 BC.

4.2 The Glory of Egyptian Civilization

By the mid-Twentieth Century BC, Egypt, the "Land of the Blacks," was the undisputed master of the ancient world. With its economic, political, military, and cultural might, it held the ancient world in awe. By technological innovation, military prowess, and shear determination, Egypt propelled its political influence all the way to the Euphrates River, into modern day Iraq.[3] Historical evidence

---

[1] Finch, *Echoes of the Old Darkland*, 123. Diop, *Civilization or Barbarism*, 17.

[2] ibid.

[3] According to Bright, Egypt's adaptation of Aryan military technology, i.e., the light horse drawn chariot and the composite bow gave the Egyptian Army unparalleled fire power and propelled Egyptian influence

suggests Egypt influenced the entire Mediterranean basin. The Mediterranean Sea literally became an Egyptian "lake." [4] Herodotus, known as the "Father of History," (485-425 BC) recorded an ancient account of Egyptian colonization of Southern Russia. His account is preserved in his *History* (See **Appendix E** on Page 156).

4.3 Rumbling in the Frozen North

There is evidence of a Black African presence in the Nile Valley region as well as Europe. If the Egyptian chronology is to be believed, their civilization goes back 39,000 years BC. The African presence in Europe dates back at least 120,000 years.[5] If this were coupled with an African presence in Asia and India, it would stand to reason

---

all the way to the Euphrates River. John Bright, *A History of Israel* (Philadelphia: Westminster Press, 1981), 108-109.

[4]There is a substantial body of research that suggests Black Egyptians had extensive contacts with Europe. Poe suggests Egypt, through its military might, imposed a rigid peace upon the entire Mediterranean region through a combination of naval and land forces from 1475-1375 BC. Poe calls this Egyptian imposed peace, the *Pax Aegyptiaca*, or "Egyptian Peace." This *Pax Aegytiaca* predated the *Pax Romana*, or "Roman Peace," by at least 1300 years and the period when Britannia (England) "ruled the waves" by at least 3000 years. The great sea-faring Black Canaanites, the Phoenicians (occupants of modern day Lebanon), working at the behest of the Egyptians, established economic interests as far away as Great Britain, through the mining of tin in modern day Cornish. The Phoenicians also built the ships used by the Egyptian navy to patrol the Mediterranean Sea. Richard Poe, *Black Spark, White Fire: Did African Explorers Civilize Ancient Europe?* (Rocklin, CA, 1997), 127-154. Diop, *Civilization or Barbarism*, 99.

[5]Finch, *Echoes of the Old Darkland*, 29.

that the family of Cush and Egypt had done quite well for themselves. The combination of a relatively peaceful environment and international stability created a near ideal situation for its inhabitants. This was about to abruptly change with the arrival of white-skinned nomadic tribes from the cold northern regions of Europe and Central Asia.

If the first inhabitants of Europe were *Black*-skinned, where did those persons with *white* skin originate? Charles S. Finch, a research physician on the faculty of Atlanta's internationally acclaimed Morehouse School of Medicine, offers a plausible explanation. Finch states:

> 1) The evolution of the Caucasoid occurred in an ice age environment near the southern limit of the great line of European glaciers in an area of southwestern Russia (Eurasia) around the 51st parallel; 2) white skin was more favorably adapted to the ecological conditions of this region during the critical period; 3) this proto-Caucasoid population experienced a prolonged period of isolation that enabled it to develop into a distinct subspecies.[6]

Finch's point, simply put, is those deemed as "Caucasoid" or "white," evolved from the *original* Humans, i.e., African migrants that arrived in Europe and settled thousands of years before. They became "white" as

---

[6]Finch, "The Evolution of the Caucasoid,"17. Also, Finch, *Echoes of the Old Darkland*, 28-29.

they adapted to their geographical as well as climatic circumstances! They are called "Caucasoid," because it seems that they originated in the rugged Caucasus Mountains of Southern Russia, otherwise known as Central Asia, hence their subsequent name *"Caucasians."*[7]

---

[7]The term "Caucasian," as a reference to the nomads that spilled out of the Caucasus Mountain Range in Central Asia, was first coined by the Eighteenth Century German anthropologist, J. Blumenbach. Rogers, *Sex and Race*, 24. Finch explains the need for the "Caucasoid" to turn white. Just as Gloger's Law dictates that mammals originating in warm climates must develop dark skin, Diop, *Civilization or Barbarism*, 11. According to Finch, Humans in frigid climates have no need for Black skin. Says Finch, "[the] northern clime with [its] many sunless days, shorter hours of day light through much of the year, [has] a more tangible angle of sunlight. In this situation, the melanin...becomes a liability because it is screening out sunlight, whose availability is drastically reduced [in the Arctic]...Since sun exposure is so severely limited at such latitudes, melanin's function of screening out ultraviolet rays to protect the skin against cancer becomes [unnecessary]. Simply put, Black skin in an ice-age type environment would become a liability rather than an asset." Finch, "The Evolution of the Caucasoid," 19. Interestingly enough, Nordic and Eskimo traditions speak of "little" Africans living in the farthest reaches of the north, i.e., Northern Europe, Greenland, the Arctic Circle, and the Northeastern coast of North America even as late as AD 1632. The Greenlanders called them the *Skaelling*, or "small." We noted earlier small Africans still populate islands off the coast of Vietnam and on certain islands in the Philippines. If this is the case, it would not be far-fetched to assume that there were "small" Africans in the far north, especially since the world's first inhabitants were Black-skinned Africans who migrated all over the world. However, if persons with white skin evolved from these first settlers, why did the Skaelling remain Black-skinned? Finch offers a plausible explanation. He suggests the Skaelling Africans were able to retain their coloration because, unlike the Africans trapped behind the ice in Central Asia, they had access to Vitamin D-laden northern salt-water fish. Finch, *Echoes of the Old Darkland*, 33-34,38-40.

As the Wurm glacial (75,000-12,000 BC) came and went,[8] this population developed in isolation to the rest of Black Humanity. Cut off from warmth and civilization, they began to spiritually merge with their environment. In the bitterly frigid northern climes of Europe and Central Asia, with its scarcity of food and shelter, they developed the necessary skills in order to survive, and obeyed a basic law—*kill or be killed.*

Their frigid environment prevented them from becoming farmers. Therefore, they lived an unsettled life.

---

[8]The Ice Age is divided into four "glacial periods." A *glacial* period is a prolonged period of cooling. In contrast, an *interglacial* period is a period when the climate warms. The Ice Age is estimated to have lasted from 1,700,000-12,000 BC, ibid., 17. Finch argues that prior to the beginning of the fourth and final glacial (The Wurm Glacial Period, 75,000-12, 000 BC). Africans had migrated to Europe (120,000-75,000 BC) and settled in around Southern Russia (Eurasia). When the temperature began to cool again (75,000-40,000) BC, these Africans were literally trapped behind the ice. After the temperature began to cool again, they began to adapt to their environment, ibid.,29-31. Diop claims that the fair-skinned tribes evolved from Black African migrants in *Western Europe,* specifically in the area of the *Pyrenees Mountain Range* of Northern Spain and Southern France in Western Europe 40,000-20,000 years ago. He thought they originated in Western Europe, and that later a branch migrated to the *Caucasus Mountain Range* in Eurasia. Diop, *Civilization or Barbarism*, 13, 18-19. Contrary to this view, there are others that believe that they evolved to their present state while in the *Caucasus Mountain Range.* Finch, "The Evolution of the Caucasiod," 17. It is really not important as to *where* they evolved. It is important to know that once they emerged from their frigid environment, they began to wreak havoc upon Egyptian and Cushite civilization through their migratory patterns and invasions.

They were wanderers, or "nomads." Whenever they did seek shelter, evidence suggests that they lived in filthy conditions, literally *underground*. In order to shield themselves from the cold, they used feces, human and animal, to block the freezing temperature. Although the eminent Roman historian, P. Cornelius Tacitus (AD 55 – 117) wrote of Aryan living conditions in Germany, his description, contained in his detailed study of Aryan barbarians entitled *Germania,* was perhaps a reflection of the way they lived while trapped behind the Eurasian ice. Says Tacitus,

> Everyone knows the tribes of Germany have no cities and that they do not even tolerate closely contiguous dwellings. They live scattered and apart, just as a spring, a meadow, or a wood has attracted them. Their villages they do not arrange in our fashion, with the buildings connected and joined together, but every person surrounds his dwelling with an open space, either as a precaution against the disasters of fire, or because they *do not know how to* build. No use is made by them of stone or tile; they employ timber for all purposes, rude masses without ornament or attractiveness. Some parts of their buildings they stain more carefully with a clay so clear and bright that it resembles painting, or a colored design. They ...dig ...[underground] caves, *and pile on [the] cave [entrances] great heaps of [human and animal feces to shelter them*

> *from winter's] cold and as a receptacle for the year's [crops].... [Italics Added].*

They did not, as a rule, raise crops; they domesticated and herded livestock, i.e., sheep, goats, cattle, and horses. They were constantly on the move looking for fresh grazing land. This meant, if necessary, violently seizing land belonging to others. Weather conditions and overgrazing dictated a constant search for vegetation for their animals. Curtis says,

> They were apparently wide ranging and, *from the standpoint of their neighbors, warlike.* In the practice of pastoral nomadism, they were compelled to seek continually for new pastures, and particularly during cycles of dry years, their capacity to move into another's territory would have been of immense survival value. [Italics Added][9]

Because their existence was so precarious, they were always on the move searching for fresh pasturage. Land seizures by *violent* conquest became virtuous and admired. The need to defend one's land, even at the cost of one's life, was thought to be the greatest good. In our time, to "die for" one's "country" inspires succeeding generations to greater acts of heroism. Bloodshed, bravery in the heat of battle, and even sacrificial death for one's comrades are virtues that our society inherited from the northern tribes.

---

[9] Curtis, *Indo-European Origins*, 37.

In fact, the only way the Viking could enter his "paradise," Valhalla, was to suffer and die a gory death on the battlefield.

Their violent, male-dominated way of life was a reflection of their environment. Finch notes:

> "...[Northern Europe and the Caucasus Mountain region were] cold, harsh [and] forbidding environments hostile to crops but supporting a nomadic lifestyle with a premium on herding, fighting, and raiding skills as small nomadic bands competed with one another for water, forage, and livestock. Therefore the masculine attribute would have been highly prized in this setting and women, poorly suited to these pursuits, would to a large extent have been reduced to [the role of child bearers and], concerned solely with domestic chores. Male status would be paramount because the lifestyle would have put a premium on combativeness, competitiveness, and indiviuality.[10]

---

[10]Finch, *Echoes of the Old Darkland*, 59-60. Renowned anthropologist, Marija Gimbutas said, "...throughout the many centuries, their continuous need for expansion fermented the psyche of vagabonds...to live by war and plunder [was] of all things most glorious." Marijas Gimbutas, "Proto-Indo-European Culture: The Kurgan Culture During the Fifth, Fourth, and Third Millennia BC." in George Cardona, ed., *Indo-European and Indo-Europeans: Papers Presentation at the University of Pennsylvania* (Philadelphia: University of Pennsylvania Press, 1970), 190.

In what could be no more than a reflection of Aryan barbarity, Tactitus describes the European barbarian's penchant for war, blood and gore in the following terms,

> When they go into battle, it is a disgrace for the chief to be surpassed in valor, [and it is] a disgrace for his followers not to equal the valor of the chief. And it is a [disgrace] to have survived the chief, and returned from the field. To defend, to protect him, to ascribe one's own brave deeds to his renown, is the height of loyalty. The chief fights for victory; his [tribal followers] fight for their chief. If their native state sinks into the [laziness] of prolonged peace ... many of its noble youths voluntarily seek those tribes which are waging some war, both because inaction is odious to their race, and because *they win renown more readily in the midst of peril, and cannot maintain a numerous following except by violence and war*. Indeed, men look to the liberality of their chief for their war-horse and their bloodstained and victorious lance. Feasts and entertainments, which, though inelegant, are plentifully furnished, are their only pay. The means of this bounty come from war and [rape]. Nor are they as easily persuaded to [farm] and to wait for the year's [crops] as to challenge an enemy and earn the honor (!) of wounds. *Nay, they actually think it tame and stupid to acquire by the sweat of toil what they might win by their blood* [Italics Added].

4.4 The Ice Melts and the World Trembles: The Assault Upon African Civilization

The Ice Age ended around 12,000 BC. Approximately four thousand years after the end of the Ice Age, around 8000 BC, a group of the white-skinned tribes moved to the farthest reaches of Northern Europe. They either moved from the Pyrennees Mountain Range located between Northern Spain and Southern France in Western Europe or from the Caucasus Mountain Range in Central Asia. From those groups sprang the Germans and Scandinavians. A group of Scandinavians moved eastward into what is now Eastern Europe. Other branches of this group migrated either to or from the Caucasus Mountain Range in Russia. Other branches moved to the river regions of the Rhine and Danube. A portion of this migratory group attempted an invasion of Egypt around 3150-3000 BC.[11] Around 2200 BC, one branch found its way to present day Greece.[12]

Approximately 7,600 years after the Wurm glacial period ended (4400 BC), migrants from the Caucasus Mountain Range began to move south into areas that had been previously all African. With the ice melting, there was nothing that could stop the advance of those tribes. From their enclaves in the Caucasus Mountains a particularly

---

[11] Curtis *Indo-European Origins*, 91

[12] Diop, *Civilization or Barbarism*, 13, 18-19. Finch, "Evolution of the Caucasoid," 17.

mobile group emerged, the *Aryans*. These persons are sometimes called "Indo-European." Their origins are shrouded in mystery, but careful research on the part of such scholars as Diop,[13] Kumar,[14] and Curtis[15] have shed light upon the Aryan past.

With the end of the Wurm glacial period, the Aryans began a long and destructive trek out of the Caucasus Mountains in three migratory waves. In each of these waves, they moved south and west.[16]

---

[13]Diop, *Civilization or Barbarism*, 18-20

[14]G.D. Kumar, "The Ethnic Components of the Builders of the Indus Valley Civilization," *Journal of Indo-European Studies* 1:1 (Spring 1973): 66-77.

[15]V.R. Curtis *Indo-European Origins*, American University Studies, Series XI, vol. 21 (New York: Peter Lang, 1988).

[16]Their migrations took them into Africa, the Near and Middle East, and what we now call "India." The migrations were thought to have occurred in the following sequence: 4400-4200 BC, 3400-3200 BC, 3000-2800 BC. ibid., 23,27. These migrants are known as Indo-Europeans. Sometimes they are designated *Aryas*, or *Aryans*. In scholarly circles, the Aryans go by many names. Some scholars call them the "Kurgan People." This is based upon their custom of burying their dead in dirt mounds called "kurgans." Curtis, *Indo-European Origins*, 18-24. "Indo" relates to one of their war gods, *Indra*. Indra's name means, "destroyer of cities." The Aryan followers of Indra invaded the Cushite Subcontinent of what is known now as India around 1550 BC, ibid., 21. "European" relates to the area they emerged from, i.e., the Caucasus Mountain Range located in Eurasia. More precisely, it relates to the area where they launched their invasion of the inhabited world after the "discovery" of America in 1492, the Continent of Europe. So as to avoid confusion, I will call these migrants, "Aryans." The name "Aryan" took on horrific connotations with the rise of Adolf Hitler's Nazi Party in the Germany of the 1930s. With his doctrine of *Aryan*

4.5 One Fell Swoop: The Destructive Occupation of Egypt

The Ice Age ended around 12,000 BC. It seems as if there was no discernable population movement on the Aryan's part to the Cushite domains, until 4400-4200 BC. Around 3150-3000 BC, the Aryans migrated in a southern direction, towards Mesopotamia, Syria, Canaan, and Egypt. Their basic intent was to find fresh pasturage for their flocks. But their very presence insured destruction and chaos. The settled Cushite civilizations were for the most part agriculturally based. These opposing lifestyles, one based upon grazing and depletion of the environment and the other based upon farming and living in harmony with the soil, were bound to clash.[17]

Around 3150-3000 BC, the Aryans struck Egypt. Their lasting influence is debateable.[18] The first reliable

---

superiority, meaning the *Aryans*, specifically its German branch, was the *"Master Race,"* he proceeded to systematically wage genocide on any group he deemed to be sub-Human. The types of individuals slated for extermination were Jews and the Slavic peoples of Eastern Europe, i.e., Russians, Ukrainians, and Georgians. Dissident Catholics and Protestants, Communists, labor activists, socialists, the disabled, homosexuals and even Jehovah's Witnesses were not exempt. When Hitler sent his military into Russia, in 1941, he proceeded to embark upon one of the greatest slaughters in Human history. Toland, *Adolf Hitler*, 896-901.

[17] Curtis, *Indo-European Origins*, 91

[18] Curtis feels that the arrival of these invaders brought about the founding of the First Dynasty, or ruling house ibid., 95. This is highly suspect. How could the arrival of these barbarians bring about "civilization"? I contend that these invaders were the first of a series of intruders that destabilized Cushite societies.

reports of Aryan invasions come from the Third Century BC Egyptian historian Manetho. Manetho writes of a tribe of invaders that came from the East. He called them the *Hyksos*, or *Shepherd Kings*. It would make sense for the Egyptians to call them *Shepherds* since, like all of these migrants from the North, they were composed of roving bands of livestock herders. The Hyksos ruled Egypt for nearly 150 years (1750 -1670 BC). It seems that they entered Egypt and conquered it without a major battle. This probably occurred during a period of Egyptian weakness.[19]

The native Egyptian rulers were driven out and sought refuge in Cush, directly to the south. This ironically empowered the Black Egyptian exiles by bonding them with their Cushite brothers. Sometime between 1675-1600 BC, a Black Egyptian commoner living in Cush, Senakhtenre Tao, rallied the Black Egyptians. Under Senakhtenre Tao, the Egyptians drove the Hyksos out of Northeastern Africa, thereby restoring Black African rule in Egypt. With Senaktenre Tao's victory, Egypt would maintain its territorial integrity for nearly 300 years.[20]

---

[19]ibid., 101. Says Manetho, "A blast of God smote us....and unexpectedly from the regions of the East, invaders of an obscure race marched in confidence to victory against our land...[t]hey seized it without striking a blow; and having overpowered the rulers of the land they then burned our cities ruthlessly, razed to the ground the temples of the gods, and treated all the natives with a cruel hostility, massacring some and leading into slavery the wives and children of others." Legrand H. Clegg II, "Black Rulers of the Golden Age," in *Egypt Revisited*, ed., Ivan Van SertimaNew Brunswick, NJ: Transaction Publishers, 1995), 241.

[20]ibid., 243.

Under the leadership of subsequent leaders, Egyptian influence extended east as far as Syria.[21]

4.6 The Invasion of the Cushite Subcontinent: Darkness Becomes Evil

The Aryan Hyksos were expelled from Black Egypt between 1675-1600 BC, by a combined Egyptian-Cushite army. By 1500 BC, another Aryan horde swung south into India.

This invasion had far more serious consequences for the children of Ham. These consequences are with us even today. Since the invaders were white, and the object of their conquest was Black, i.e., the Cushites; *Black* was equated with *evil* and *white* with *good*. Hood correctly observes how the effects of the Aryan conquest are felt in India even to this day. Hood says,

> In India, Blackness is generally undesirable as a sign of beauty. This disdain for Blackness has deep cultural roots that may trace back to the early battles in ancient India of the 1500s BC between the *Aryas* (Aryans) the original light skinned invaders and conquerors of North West India (Punjab) and the *Dasas* or *Dasyo*-the original dark skinned inhabitants.[22]

---

[21]Curtis, *Indo-European Origins*, 102
[22]Hood, *Begrimed and Black*, 4. Hood also gives an extended summary of the negative racial attitudes towards people of African descent,

With the view that the color Black as being "evil" and white being "good," it is no wonder the Rabbis, starting in the Third Century AD, construed the color of *Ham* (translated from the Hebrew as *Black*) as being *evil*. It is a wonder, though, as to how they construed Noah's anger at Ham and Canaan as a curse upon an entire portion of Humanity. An even bigger mystery is how they matched the physical characteristics of African people with being cursed, i.e., skin color, lip size, eye color, hair texture, etc. It could be argued that the **Biblical** *text* was a mere pre-*text* or *excuse* for subjugating the African.

---

in Middle Eastern, Asian and European societies, towards Blackness in his Introduction to *Begrimed and Black*, 1-21. The Euro-American view of Blackness was influenced by the Aryan view. In non-African societies, *Blackness* is equated with *evil*. A typical definition of the color Black goes like this, "Black"...the *opposite of white*... especially ...Negro...totally without light...soiled; dirty...wicked, *evil*, harmful, ...*disgraceful*...full of sorrow; sad; dismal; gloomy; sullen; angry; ...without hope, a *Black* villain, complete darkness and the absence of light. The definition rendered for *white* goes as follows, "...having the color of *pure* snow or *milk*;...the opposite of *Black*...morally or spiritually *pure*; *spotless*....free from *evil* intent...having a light-colored skin; Caucasoid...honest or honorable and fair...happy and fair. David B. Guralnik, ed., *Webster's New World Dictionary of the American Language*, 2nd. Edition (New York: World Publishing, 1972), 146, 1621. On a day when something horrible occurs it is usually called "*Black* Tuesday, *Black* Wednesday, etc. Mourning clothes are usually *Black*. Illegal activities are dubbed "*Black*, " i.e., *Black* mail, *Black* market, etc. The plague that swept Europe in the Fourteenth Century, destroying nearly a quarter of that continent's population is called the *Black* Plague. To exclude a person or group from an activity means to *Black*ball the excluded parties. People with evil intent have *Black* hearts.

4.7 The Tribes Look to the West: Egypt Under Attack

Aryan successes in India encouraged more intrusions into the Cushite dominions. In the 1600s BC, a particularly aggressive band of Aryans, the Hittites, cast their eyes upon Canaan and Africa. They took aim at Egypt, which was weak and divided under Hykso rule. The Hittites were united under the leadership of a certain Taberna (1680-1650 BC). Under Taberna's successors, the Hittites put tremendous pressure on Syria, the eastern outpost of the Egyptian empire.[23] By 1594 BC, the Hittites invaded Mesopotamia and sacked the Cushite city of Babylon.[24] After expelling the Hyksos, only stubborn resistance on the part of the Black Egyptians kept the barbarians from taking all of Syria and Canaan and threatening Egypt itself. Egypt was saved, but at a terrible price, its control of Canaan was severely curtailed.

---

[23] Curtis, *Indo-European Origins*, 105. Also, Bright, *A History of Israel*, 109. The "Hittites," according to the Table of Nations were descended from Cush (**Genesis 10:15**). If they descended from Cush, how could they be Aryan? As the Aryans advanced, they took on the historical, political and cultural trappings of the countries they occupied. Cushites had migrated all over the ancient world and occupied substantial tracts of land, including the "Land of the Hittites," which was none other than modern day Turkey. If the Hyksos could consider themselves "Egyptians," why could not the ancient Aryan occupants in the region of modern day Turkey consider themselves "Hittites?" The present day Arab occupants of Egypt classify themselves as the direct descendants of the [ancient *European*] Egyptians. It is considered insulting to call or classify them as "Africans."

[24] Curtis, *Indo-European Origins*, 105.

4.8 The First Cold War: Black Egypt Faces Off With the Hittites

Not only was Egyptian control of Canaan compromised, but also both the Egyptians and Hittites possessed "super-power" status. The Hittites were the aggressors, but they faced a determined foe in the Egyptians. Canaan then became a pawn between the two powers. Neither empire had the power to inflict a death blow upon the other, but the state of "Cold War" that existed between the two empires ruined Canaan's economy and caused the population of the region to drop by nearly half. By the 1400s BC, Pharaoh Thutmoses III (1484-1462 BC) reasserted Egyptian control over portions of Canaan.[25]

Through periodic armed invasion and practicing the policy of "divide and rule," Egypt's ruler, Thutmoses III, diminished Hittite influence in the region. Coote says:

> Besides plundering [Canaanite] cities, and carrying away captives (including hostages from leading families), military equipment, precious objects, grain, and livestock, the Egyptian conquerors required annual tribute in agricultural produce, as well as other provisions, [forced] labor, and military service. They established a network of

---

[25]Not only did Thutmoses III aggressively confront the Hittites, he extended Egyptian authority throughout the entire Eastern Mediterranean area. Egyptian rule extended from the islands of Crete and Cyprus in the west, to Babylon in the east. Diop, *The African Origin of Civilization*, 209.

garrison cities in [Canaan] that also served as depots for the grain and provisions going to support Egyptian power at home and abroad.[26]

The late Fourteenth Century BC witnessed the renewal of active hostilities between the Egyptians and the Hittites. Nearly 100 years later, because of the decisive and brilliant military leadership of Rameses II, Hittite power was finally broken after a decisive battle at Kadesh-on-the -Orantes River (Syria) in 1285.[27]

---

[26]Coote, *Power, Politics, and the Making of the **Bible**.*, 20

[27] ibid., 109.

[28]Curtis, *Indo-European Origins*, 106

4.9 Storms Arrive From the West: The Arrival Of the Sea Peoples

At the beginning of the 1200s BC, Egypt was under attack. Not from the East, but from a group of Aryans that came from the Mediterranean Island of Crete. Since they were seafarers, the Egyptians called them the *Sea Peoples*.[28]

The Sea Peoples attempted to invade Egypt twice between 1220-1150 BC. The first attempted invasion occurred in 1220 BC, approximately 20 years after the **Exodus**. The group that attempted this invasion was called the *Peleset*. Curtis believes that the Peleset are the **Biblical Philistines**.[29]

The second attempted invasion occurred during the reign of Rameses III (1194 -1162 BC), the Sea Peoples again attempted to invade Egypt. Around 1186 BC, great land and sea battles occurred as Egypt fought for its very existence. The combined land and amphibious assaults dwarfed such Twentieth Century battles as Verdun (World War I) and Normandy (World War II) in their ferocity. The

---

[29] ibid.

invaders were repulsed,[30] but at great cost. The cost was two-fold. First, though Egypt was safe, the war exacted a heavy toll on its resources. Second, the Sea People were expelled but fell back into an enclave in Canaan out of the reach of a weakened Egypt. This turn of events caused Egyptian-Cushite civilization to take on a defensive stance. The Sea People had been repulsed from Africa, but at the cost of weakening Egyptian control over Canaan. These "Peleset," or Philistines, set up five city-states in Canaan, Gaza, Ahkalon, Ashdod, Ekron, and Gath. Their presence in Canaan had such a tremendous impact that their name was lent to the region and Canaan came to be known as Palestine. The Philistines harassed the Israelites (**Judges 14-16, 1 Samuel 4-7:1-17, 13, 14:1-23, 17, 31**), until David completed his savage, but effective, campaign to absorb the Philistines into his empire, around 1000 BC (**2 Samuel 5:17-25**).

4.10 Chapter Summary

Migrating tribes, originating in the Caucasus Mountain Range approximately 7,600 years after the Ice Age ended, swept through areas of the world that had been under the control and cultivation of the children of Ham for several thousand years.

The success of Ham's children in protecting their heritage was a somewhat checkered affair. In the case of the Subcontinent, it became "India," and Canaan became

---

[30] ibid.

"Palestine."[31] In the case of Egypt and Cush, their territorial integrity was maintained in Africa, but at the cost of diminished political, cultural, and military influence throughout the world.

The Egyptians and Cushites remained powers in North Africa, but they would never attempt direct military intervention in the region for several hundred years. After the rise of the Assyrians, Egypt would decline into an abysmal state of affairs until it nearly lost its Black African identity.[32]

---

[31] The land came to be known as *Syria Palistina* after the Jews failed in their second attempt to dislodge the Romans from their land during the Bar Kosiba Revolt (AD 132-135), Coote, *Power, Politics and the Making of the Bible*, 123.

[32] Egypt was able to maintain its national borders after ejecting the Sea Peopl; however, things would never be the same. Six hundred years after the expulsion of that group of invaders, the Assyrians attacked and sacked Thebes in 663 BC. From then on, a series of invasions and occupations diluted Egypt's Blackness. These groups invaded and debased the population in the following order: Assyria 720-663 BC; Babylon 660-539 BC; Persia 536-331 BC; the Greeks, beginning with Alexander the Great 332-31 BC; the Romans 31 BC-324 AD; the Byzantine Romans AD 324-650; the Arabs AD 650-1517; the Ottoman Turks 1517-1840; and finally the British 1882-1922. During the mid-1800s, direct Turkish rule over Egypt was weakened due to local Turkish officials assuming more authority for themselves. One such ruler was an Albanian named Ishmael Pasha. Pasha was more of a bungler than statesman. Delusional to the extreme, he incompetently "governed" Egypt from 1863-1879. He made a disastrous bid to transform Egypt into a *European* country. His policies were based upon delusion than substance. He attempted to "modernize" Egypt by constructing an opera house, paving a few roads, and constructing rail transportation. His rather amateurish efforts at aping European "progress" bankrupted the country and provided the British with a pretext to occupy the country from the late 1880s well into the Twentieth Century. Ishmael Pasha

Even as Egyptian and Cushite civilization's grandeur would be diminished, they were about to enter another arena of history. This arena would involve taking in and giving shelter to a wandering band of shepherds.

---

even attempted an invasion of Ethiopia in an attempt to create a neo-Egyptian empire. The attempt came in the form of a series of armed incursions into Ethiopia by Egyptian forces equipped and trained along European lines (1875-76). Several former officers of the Confederate Army, veterans of the American southern state's war of rebellion (1861-1865), led one of the invading columns. The Egyptians, trained and led in part by the Confederate veterans, suffered a humiliating defeat at the Battle of Gura (March 1876) Bahru Zewde, *A History of Modern Ethiopia, 1855-1974* (Addis Abba, Ethiopia: Addis Ababa University Press, 1991), 45, 47, 50-53. Prior to Ishmael Pasha's crushing defeat at the hands of the Ethiopians, he foolishly declared, "My country is now in *Europe*; it is no longer in *Africa*." [Italics added]. Fouad Ajami "The Sorrows of Egypt," *Foreign Affairs*, 74:5 (September/October 1995):83. Egypt's "European" identity is so entrenched that, the United States Department of State considers Egypt a "white" country.

4.11 Suggestions For Further Reading

Arvidsson, Stefan. "Aryan Mythology as Science and Ideology," *Journal of the American Academy of Religion*, 67:2 (June 1999): 327-354.

Baddeley, John F. *The Rugged Flanks of the Caucasus*, Vol. 2. London: Oxford University Press, 1940.

Dawkins, W. Boyd. *Cave Hunting, Researches on the Evidence of Caves, Respecting the Early Inhabitants Of Europe.* London: Macmillan & Co., 1874.

Gimbutas, Marija "Old Europe c. 7000-3500 BC: The Earliest Infiltration of the Indo-European Peoples," *Journal of Indo-European Studies*, 1:1 (Spring 1973) : 1-20.

Schrader, O. *Prehistoric Antiquities of the Aryan Peoples* trans. Frank Byron Jfvons London: Griffin & Co., 1890.

Pritchard, James B. ed., *The Ancient Near East: An Anthology of Texts*, Vol. 1, Princeton, NJ: Princeton University Press, 1957.

_____.*The Ancient Near East: A New Anthology of Texts*, Vol. 2, Princeton, NJ: Princeton University Press, 1975.

Velikovsky, Immanuel. *Ages in Chaos*. New York: Doubleday & Co., 1952.

Williams, Chancellor. *The Destruction of Black Civilization :Great Issues of a Race From 4500 BC to 2000 AD*. Chicago: Third World Press, 1987.

113

> "...the Egyptians are no longer [to be] deliberately confused with the Indo-Europeans or Semites, but ranked in the great family of Ham and Canaan, in conformity with the Biblical text."

Cheikh Anta Diop
Anthropologist

CHAPTER 5

Abraham's Family and Egypt's Hospitality

5.1 Chapter Introduction

Despite Egypt's setbacks and being forced out of Southern Russia and Mesopotamia, it retained enough power to maintain its position in Africa. Egypt witnessed its influence diminish in Canaan over a one thousand-year period beginning with the invasions by the northern tribes. Egypt was able to defend its borders, but its one-sided control over the region ceased after the expulsion of the Sea Peoples in the 1200s and 1100s BC.

As Egypt's influence steadily diminished, its civilizing presence was lost, along with its military power, in such regions such as Mesopotamia, and Southern Russia. A group of Aryans, the Hurrians, migrated south and west out of the Caucasus Mountain region, around 2400 BC,[1] they began to put pressure on Cushite Mesopotamia, causing massive social dislocation and disruption.[2] The Hurrian invasion created a massive population shift from Mesopotamia to the west thereby causing a sizeable

---

[1] Curtis, *Indo-European Origins*, 100.

[2] Bright, *A History of Israel*, 61-64.

number of Mesopotamian Cushites to move in a westerly direction towards Canaan.

5.2 Uprooted But Called: Abraham's Family and Their Journey West

One of the chief cities of Mesopotamia was Ur,[3] the ancestral home of Abraham (in **Genesis** *Abraham* is known as *Abram* until **Genesis 17:5**). It is the story of Abraham, God's promise to him, and his family's stay, as well as expulsion from Egypt, nearly 500 years later that will occupy our attention.

The exact date of Abraham's departure from Ur is forever lost to us. At best we can say he appears on the scene 1950-1750 BC.[4] Around 2400 BC, approximately

---

[3]The **Bible** says nothing more about this great Cushite city, except in a passing reference to Abraham and his family. It only tells us that Ur was his ancestral home. It also tells us that Abraham's father, Terah, gathered his family and headed west in the direction of Canaan. However, Terah only made it as far as Haran in Syria, there he died. Subsequently Abraham received a call from the LORD to leave Haran and migrate to Canaan (**Genesis 11:31, 12:1-5**). Although the **Bible** uses Ur as a reference point for Abraham's family, Ur was a place of tremendous importance in the ancient world. Ur, between 3000-2000 BC, served as an important stop over point on the trade route between the Indus Valley, Canaan and Africa. Jean-Cl. Margueron, "Ur," in *The Anchor Bible Dictionary*. Mesopotamia was a *region* encompassing the Tigris and Euphrates Rivers. The region's centers of influence were its cities, of which Ur was one. Last, according to the **Bible**, a few of these cities were Babylon, Erech. Akkad, and Calneh. Those cities were founded by one of Cush's sons, Nimrod (**Genesis 10:10**).

[4]Marshall, *A Guide Through the Old Testament*, 13.

800 years prior to Egypt's Hykso era, the Hurrians, began a slow but destructive encroachment upon Cushite Mesopotamia. According to Bright, the Hurrians were of the same stock that eventually invaded and plundered the Cushite civilizations located on the Subcontinent during the 1500s BC. This branch of the Aryan tribes began its destructive invasion of Mesopotamia around 2400 BC with the destruction of Cushite Akkad.[5]

By Abraham's time, the northern tribes threatened Mesopotamian cities such as Ur. This set in motion one of the greatest forced migrations and dislocations the ancient world had seen. Entire populations were uprooted, as in the case of the Amorites. It is thought that Abraham was an Amorite.

Of course, we take it that the call of Abraham is genuine. The LORD called him to leave Haran for the purpose of serving as a blessing to all people (**Genesis 12:1-3**). But prior to his stay in Haran, he was a resident of Ur. As a resident of Ur, he might have been witness to the

---

[5] Akkad was founded by Nimrod, one of Ham's grandsons (**Genesis 10:10**). Marshall, *A Guide Through the Old Testament*, 62. Copher, basing his observations upon the work of Marcel Dieulafoy A.H. Sayce, concluded that the original inhabitants of the region were Cushite. The basis for this claim is their ancient designation as "the Black-headed race." If this were true, then the great lawgiver/king, Hammurabi 1848-1792 BC?) whose great "Code," predated the Ten Commandments by several hundred years would have had to be Black-skinned. Copher, "Blacks/Negroes: Participants," 37. The Hurrian devastation of some areas of Mesopotamia was so complete, between 2300-2200 BC, several cities were actually leveled to the ground. Gimbutas, "Proto-Indo-European Culture," 186.

horrible destruction wrought by the northern tribes. If this is true, it is highly unlikely that his clan traveled from Ur to Canaan alone. The roads to Canaan may have been clogged with Cushite refugees fleeing west towards Canaan and the relative safety of Africa.

5.3 *Abraham, His Family and His Wanderings*

Abraham's call, combined with the massive population shift caused by the northern tribes, had literally uprooted him from the urban environment of Mesopotamia. This caused him to become a wanderer. During this wandering phase, Abraham's family began to be referred to as "Hebrew[s]" (**Genesis 14:13**). The name "Hebrew" may derive from the Canaanite view of Abraham's family. The word occurs in some Canaanite texts as *'abiru*, meaning "wanderer" or "outsider." The Canaanites may have given Abraham's family this designation because, in contrast to the Canaanites, they lived in the wilderness instead of cities.[6]

Though Abraham was not an Aryan, their disruptive presence probably caused him, as well as other Cushite Mesopotamians, to adopt a semi-Aryan lifestyle. As the Aryans destroyed everything in their path, by default, those who survived their destruction lost everything and devolved to the level of rootless wanderers. Perhaps the most obvious adaptation to their way of life was Abraham's family adopting the lifestyle of wealthy nomadic livestock

---

[6]Marshall, *A Guide Through the Old Testament*, 34

herders.[7] As the Aryans fought over grazing land, Abraham's family feuded in the same manner (**Genesis 13:7**).[8]

Another similarity with the Aryans was Abraham's *patriarchal* lifestyle. Diop raises several points that describe the patriarchal lifestyle.

---

[7]According to Curtis, the wandering nomad could easily increase his wealth due to his ability to continuously move on to greener pastures. The only limitations placed on him were those of over-grazing. The constant search for grazing land solved this problem. His wealth was then reflected in the size of his flocks. Curtis, *Indo-European Origins*, 33. Compare this with the **Genesis** account of Abraham's wealth increasing due to Egyptian generosity, "[Pharaoh] treated [Abraham] well for [Sarah's] sake, and [Abraham] acquired *sheep and cattle* (**Genesis 12:16**)," also see **Genesis 30:25-43**. Also, **Job's** wealth was *not* measured in *currency*. He was viewed as being *wealthy* because he owned 7000 sheep, 3000, camels, 1000 head of cattle, and 500 donkeys. The author of **Job** observed that this made **Job** the wealthiest man in his region (**Job 1:3, 42:12**).

[8]The fighting between the herdsman of Lot and Abraham was more than a mere family feud. For nomads seeking to feed their flocks, even family ties meant nothing. Nomads are compelled to constantly be on the move in search for pasturage for their flocks, especially during dry years. It is only natural that they would move into another's territory if the situation warranted. According to Curtis, "...we need not look too deeply to recognize that a herd of cattle represents an enormous amount of wealth on the hoof. Such portable wealth requires a need to defend it, and even grazing rights for specific areas can become the subject of fierce contention." Curtis, *Indo-European Origins*, 36-37. Also see **Exodus 2:17**.

Among his descriptors, the following points are relevant to our discussion:

- They were nomadic (**Genesis 12:4-8**).

- The husband has the absolute right of life and death over his wife and children (**Genesis 19:6-8, Judges 11:30-39, 19:23-29**).

- Inheritance is transmitted through the father or "patriarch" [9] (**Genesis 27, 49:1-27**). [Biblical references mine].

Other characteristics of the patriarchal lifestyle should be mentioned. The eldest male in the family was the "head

---

[9] Diop, *Civilization or Barbarism*, 112-113. The founding heads of the various clans and families that eventually became the "Israel" of the **Old Testament** are often called "the Patriarchs." They are Abraham, Isaac, and Jacob. They also traditionally include ten of Jacob's sons and two of his grandsons. The **Bible** *never* refers to these men as "Patriarchs." They are identified as such because they lived a patriarchal *lifestyle*. The word derives, in part, from an Indo-European word for "father." This word appears in several Indo-European language groups: *father*=English, *Vater*=German, *fader*=Gothic, *pater*=Latin, *pate'r*=Greek, *pita'r*=Sanskrit, *pedar*=Iranian. Curtis, *Indo-European Origins*, 12. The word "patriarch," derives, in part, from two Greek words, *pate'r* (father) and *archein* (to rule). The dynamics of patriarchy are alive and well in our time. Germans often call their country the "*Father*land." Persons that possess a high degree of "love" for their country are called "*patriots*." The President of the United States was often portrayed, to Nineteenth Century Native Americans, as the "Great White *Father* in Washington." Until recently, members of city councils in American cities were called the "City *Fathers*." George Washington is often called the "*Father* of his country." The authors of the Declaration of Independence (1776), and the United States Constitution (1787), are often called America's Founding *Fathers*.

of the household." The "head" held absolute authority over all members of the household. This included authority over the lives of grown children. The patriarch could even choose his child's spouse **(Genesis 23:1-5)** and could also bind the allegiance of the family to a particular god. Both **Old** and **New Testaments** allude to this practice **(Joshua 24:15 and Acts 16:31)**.

5.4 Abraham's Family and Their Relationships With the Canaanites and the Egyptians

The **Biblical** record gives us tantalizing hints concerning Abraham's relationship with the Canaanites. Neither he nor his family would "settle" anywhere, with the exception of his nephew Lot **(Genesis 13)**. **Genesis** informs us that Lot opted to abandon the life of a nomad for that of a city dweller after his herdsmen and those of his uncle, Abraham, argued over grazing rights **(Genesis 13:5-13)**. Throughout **Genesis**, there are only two occasions where we see Abraham or his family members deviate from the nomadic life. In one instance, land is purchased **(Genesis 23)**; in that case, it was for a burial plot for Abraham's deceased wife, Sarah. In the other, soil is tilled by Isaac **(Genesis 26:12)**. Otherwise, Abraham's family *wandered* throughout Canaan and Egypt.

From time to time, the family came into contact with Egyptian and Canaanite royalty **(Genesis 12:10-20, 14, 20)**. In some cases, it was due to famine **(Genesis 12:10, 42-**

50). In other cases, it was because Abraham's sizable household included a large contingent of armed men. The armed members of Abraham's household had the capacity to tip the scales in favor of the side he chose in the event of a military conflict (**Genesis 14**).

Says Curtis,

> For pastoral nomads to mobilize in their own defense or to go to war required little more than a decision. The training and equipment was always at hand. Such peoples ...require a strong defense for their existence....Decisions must be made rapidly by relatively few people and then translated into action.[10]

Famine was a constant threat to his family's survival. In the case of famine, the family usually journeyed to the ancient world's breadbasket, Egypt (**Genesis 12:10**, and **43-50**). A primary reason for this was Abraham's nomadic lifestyle. Since his flocks and herds were dependent on fresh pasturage, during times of famine or drought, Abraham's family faced a simple choice, go to Africa and replenish their food stocks, or starve in the Canaanite wilderness. In the ancient world, Egypt's wealth, power, culture and abundant food supply attracted the nomadic tribes. Due to the advanced nature of Egyptian and Cushite civilization, it is no wonder Abraham and eventually his grandchildren would turn to Black Africa in their desperate

---

[10] ibid., 36

bid to keep from starving. Although Bishop William LaRue Dillard, a Baptist pastor, as well as scholar of rare objectivity, speaks of events relating to the descent of Joseph, his father Jacob, and that of his brothers into Egypt as they sought to escape the ravages of famine (**Genesis 43-50**), he could have just as easily been speaking of Abraham or his son, Isaac.

Dillard says,

> In ancient times, there was a steady ...relationship amongst the Black people of Africa and Israel. The ancient Israelite's civilization was [inferior in] comparison to the neighboring [Africans]. [The Africans] were at the height of their glory when the Hebrew[s] ... chose to reside in Egypt. [11]

This trend continued and accelerated as time wore on. It would ultimately have a devastating effect upon the native Black populaton.[12] However, since Egypt had pioneered advanced agricultural techniques, it served as a

---

[11]Dillard, ***Biblical*** *Ancestry Voyage*, 44-45

[12]Diop reminds us, "...the whole of Egyptian history...shows a mixture of the early population with white nomadic elements, [they came as either] conquerors or merchants. [They gradually] became increasingly important as the end of Egyptian history approached. Diop, *The African Origin of Civilization*, 4-5. This is not to say that Abraham's family was white, after all, they had come from the Cushite domain of Mesopotamia. But it could be suggested that Cushites like Abraham as well as Aryans were attracted to Egypt for different reasons. Abraham's family would frequent Egypt for food. The Aryans came for conquest.

magnet for starving nomads such as Abraham and his descendants on several occasions **(Genesis 12:10, and 43-50)**.

Though this specific passage speaks of an occurrence two generations later, **Genesis 41:54-56** is explicit in its recognition of Egypt's vital role in preventing starvation in the ancient world.

- **41:54-55**, The entire region, North Africa as well as Canaan, experienced a famine. It seems that at the beginning of the crises, Egypt had enough food to at least feed itself. Joseph, due to his high rank within the Egyptian government, had been placed in charge of food distribution.
- **41:56**, Due to Joseph's administrative skill, though Egypt's harvest was poor, he had filled food storage lockers prior to the famine. Egypt's superior food stocks then began to draw starving people throughout the region to Egypt.

According to **Genesis**, Abraham's family sojourned in Egypt twice. Both visits were necessitated by famine. The first visit was temporary **(Genesis 13:1)**; it occurred c.1750. The second lasted from c.1670 BC **(Genesis 37, 39-50)**, until the **Exodus** c.1240 BC **(Exodus 1-15)**. If the timing of our dates is correct, it is safe to say that Abraham arrived in the area of Egypt and Canaan around 1750 BC. This would have placed him in the area around the time of Hykso rule over Egypt. His nomadic lifestyle may have been a reason for his initial welcome in Egypt. In fact it seems that the only reason he was ejected was due to his dishonesty (**Genesis 12:14-20**).

5.5 Egypt's Influence Upon Abraham's Family

After Abraham's expulsion from Egypt, he would have no recorded contact with that country. Famine drove his grandson (Jacob), great grandchildren, and other members of the household, seventy in all, around 1670 BC (**Exodus 1:1-5**), back to Africa to prevent their utter starvation (**Genesis 42-50**).

According to **Exodus 12:40**, Abraham's family remained in Egypt for 430 years. After the LORD freed them from Egyptian slavery, the **Bible** informs us that their number had increased to at least 600,000 (See **Numbers 1**). How could this be? How could Abraham's family increase to such a number? The answer may lay in the probability of intermarriage between Israelites and Egyptians. There are several recorded instances of inter-marriage. There is the instance of Joseph marrying Asenath, the daughter of Potiphera, Priest of On (**Genesis 41:45**). Another recorded instance is the unnamed Cushite wife of Moses (**Numbers 12:1**). The passage relating to Abraham fathering a child by his Egyptian slave does not relate to the events recorded in **Genesis 37, 39-50** or **Exodus 1-15**, however, these passages bear witness to the suggestion that there was a great deal of intermingling between Israelites and Egyptians.

Since Abraham's family's stay in Egypt lasted almost four and a half centuries, they may have entered Egypt as a small band of *nomads*, by the time they left they were very much *African*. Their Africanity could be measured by more than skin color. It could be argued that they were also the recipients of Egypt's culture and civilization. The Africanization process is hinted at in **Genesis 41:45**. In that passage Joseph is given the Egyptian name Zaphenath-Paneah. Other Egyptian names were, Moses, Aaron, and Phineas.[12] It is obvious that the Israelites absorbed a great deal of Egypt's rich legacy of science and technology. The writer of **The Acts of the Apostles** records an obviously ancient tradition, coming from the mouth of one of the early deacons of the church, Stephen. According to **Acts 7:22**, "...Moses was trained in *all* the wisdom of the Egyptians."[13] [Italics Added]

---

[12]Coote, *Power, Politics, and the Making of the Bible*, 22. The **Book of Exodus** is explicit in showing the practice of giving Hebrew children African names. In **Exodus 2:10**, the Hebrew baby rescued from the Nile by an Egyptian princess is given the African name, *Moses*. Add to this list of African names, Assir (**Exodus 6:24**) and Pashur (**1 Chronicles 9:12**) Soggin, *A History of Ancient Israel*, 110.

[13]Just what was *all* of the wisdom of the Egyptians? Their scientific innovations and contributions are too numerous to list here, however, they are responsible for the following: the lever, Geometry, Algebra, Arithmetic, Astronomy, Medicine (Egyptian physicians were specialist in the modern sense of the word according to the ancient historian Herodotus. I included his comments on Egyptian medicine in **Appendix D**), Chemistrynote the relationship between the word *chemistry* and *Cham*—the word *Kemet*) and Architecture are Egyptian innovations. One of the "wonders" of the ancient, as well as modern, world are the Pyramids. The design of the Pyramids is so complex that it is impossible to slip a razor blade between the stones. The stones weight up to fifty tons apiece! Diop, *Civilization or Barbarism*, 231-

Abraham's descendants may have come to Egypt as starving nomads; however, they left as Africans. They intermarried with the Egyptians. They had Egyptian names. They learned science and technology from their Egyptian hosts.

5.6 Israel's Enslavement and Exodus[14]

The central theme in Israel's relationship with the LORD was the **Exodus** event. This event was not just an occurrence; it was *the* defining moment in Israel's relationship with the LORD. It was rooted in the LORD's Covenant with Abraham (**Genesis 12:1-3, 15, 17**).

The relationship established with Abraham by the LORD was maintained throughout their Canaanite wanderings, the Egyptian captivity, and their Wilderness

---

307. Many Greeks received instruction in Egyptian arts and sciences and, in due course, transmitted much of what they learned to Greece and eventually Rome. There would be no Western "civilization," had not Greece transmitted what it learned in Egypt to Europe. Black Egypt has never been given credit for its ingenuity. For the most part, historians overlook the West's debt to Africa. As he summarized this debt, George G.M. James went so far as to claim Europe and America had basically *stolen* its civilization from Egypt. Hence the title of his book, *Stolen Legacy*. George G.M. James, *Stolen Legacy* (Philosophical Library: New York, 1954).

[14] I will not give an exhaustive survey of Egyptian/Israelite relations in this section. This would take us too far afield. I recommend Bishop Dunston's *The Black Man in the Old Testament and its World*. In **Chapters 9-10**, he gives easy to read, yet concise, summaries of African/Israelite relations from the **Exodus**, through the arrival of the Greeks under the leadership of Alexander the Great in the 300s BC.

period (**Exodus 15-40, Leviticus, Numbers, and Deuteronomy**). It continued to reassert itself throughout the conquest (**Joshua**), and Settlement (**Judges**) eras. Whenever the LORD wanted to assert His ownership of Israel, He would invoke the obligatory loyalty of Israel to Him due to their deliverance from Egyptian slavery. He would remind Israel through the preamble to the Ten Commandments (**Exodus 20:2**), through the words of Joshua (**Joshua 24:4-7**), and through His resignation to Israel's rebellion (**1 Samuel 8:8**). He would also yearn for reconciliation with Israel and a return to the early days of their relationship after the **Exodus (Hosea 2:15)**.

In fact, the Egyptian period (**Genesis 37, 39-50, Exodus 1-15**) was so central to Israel's understanding of itself, that the writer of **Deuteronomy 26:1-8** instructed the Israelites to show their gratitude towards the LORD in reference to their ancestor's African experience.

A close examination of **Deuteronomy 26:1-8** reveals the impact of the Egyptian experience upon the people of Israel.

- **26:1-4** presupposes an attitude of gratitude on the part of the Israelites due to the LORD making good on His promise to Abraham through the **Exodus (Exodus 1-15)**.

- In **26:5,** the grateful Israelite repeats the sacred history. It speaks of the nomadic or "wandering," Aramean. He is called an Aramean, based upon the reference of Abraham beginning his trek to Canaan from the city named for his brother in Aram, Haran (**Genesis 11:31**). The Aramean is Abraham's grandson, Jacob. Jacob and his household went to Egypt to escape starvation.

- **26:6-8** reminds the Israelite that the Egyptians treated their ancestors harshly and that it was the LORD's power that delivered them from slavery.

What caused the relationship between Israel and Egypt to deteriorate to the level of slave and master? The **Bible** gives only the sparest details as to how this occurred. Most people are familiar with the **Exodus** story. The details contained in **Exodus 1-15** have been told and retold for centuries. The **Book of Exodus** provides, the barest of details as to why the Israelites were enslaved.

Exodus merely states,

- **1:6-7**, Joseph and his generation died, and the Israelite population began to grow at, what the Egyptian government felt was, an alarming rate.

- **1:8-10**, A new king, who did not have the same level of commitment to the Israelites came to power and convinced the Egyptians that the Israelites were a grave threat to Egypt's national security.

- **1:11-14,** the Israelites become slaves in Egypt. It seems that their main purpose was to provide labor for Egyptian public works projects. It also seems as if they were forced to work in the "fields," (agricultural production?)

A careful reconstruction of the history of Egypt during its "time of trouble" may provide a key to understanding the reason for the drastic action taken by the Egyptian authorities in **Exodus 1:6-11.**

Look at the following factors:

- The nomadic Aryans began to migrate out of the Caucasus Mountains approximately 7,600 years after the end of the Ice Age looking grazing land. Their invasive activities occurred in three waves (4400-4200 BC, 3400-3200 BC, and 3000-2800 BC). These Aryan population movements constituted their main thrusts south and west into the warmer regions controlled by Ham's family. Of course, there would be subsequent attacks upon the Cushite south by the northerners, i.e., the Hyksos, Hittites, Sea Peoples, etc., but these attacks would be from their newly acquired territories in such places as Europe and Asia.

- Around 3150-3000 BC, there is thought to have been an attempt on the part of the northern tribes to conquer Egypt.

- By the 1700s BC, the Hyksos, or *Shepherd Kings*, raped, looted, and plundered their way to power in Egypt and caused the native rulers to flee to Cush in the South.

- Around 1600-1500 BC, the Hyksos had been forced out with the aid of a sizable Cushite army.

- From about 1650-1274 BC, Egypt sparred with the Aryan Hittite Empire for control of Canaan.

- After expelling the Hyksos and fighting off the Hittites, the presence of a large body of non-Egyptians, such as the Israelites, could have fueled Egyptian paranoia towards foreigners. This could have counted for the Pharaoh saying, "the people of Israel are too many and too mighty for us. We must deal with them in a wise manner! If we don't, they will multiply in numbers, and should we have to go to war, they will join our enemies *and fight against us* and in due course—escape!" (**Exodus 1:9-10**).

- In 1220 BC and 1186 BC, the Egyptians repulsed, at great costs, invasions of Aryans known as the "Sea People." The Sea People were defeated. However, they moved to Canaan where their presence compromised Egypt's control of that region.

If Abraham arrived in Canaan sometime between 1950-1750 BC, it would place his arrival in the area of Egypt and Canaan around the time of the Aryan Hyksos' rule over Northeastern Africa. This was during a time when the Hyksos ruled Canaan by default, since Canaan was part of Egypt's imperial domain. He could have initially received a warm welcome in Egypt, without lying about Sarah's relationship to him (**Genesis 12:10-13**). Even after his lie was discovered, Abraham was allowed to keep the ample supply of food and provisions given to him by the Egyptians after he and his family were ejected from Egypt (**Genesis 12:10-20**). The warmth of his welcome and the providing of supplies and slaves could have been due to his nomadic lifestyle's similarity to the Hyksos' non-African lifestyle.

His son, Isaac, continued to live as a nomad in the land of Canaan. The LORD explicitly ordered him not to go to Egypt, but to remain in Canaan, despite a famine (**Genesis 26:3**).

According to **Genesis 43:1**, there arose a famine in Canaan (*this famine is the reference to starvation contained in* ***Deuteronomy 26****, Jacob/Israel is the wandering Aramean*). This caused Abraham's clan to return to Egypt, this time under the leadership of his grandson, Jacob (*also known as Israel, see **Genesis 32:28***). Their safety and security was guaranteed by one of Abraham's great-grandsons, Joseph. Earlier, Joseph's brothers had sold him into slavery (**Genesis 37:12-36**). Through Divine intervention, he was elevated to a position roughly equal to that of a Prime Minister **(Genesis 41:41-45)** after being falsely accused of attempted rape and serving time in an Egyptian penitentiary **(Genesis 39-40)**. Joseph's elevation kept the Israelites from starving to death.

Again, Abraham's family's initial welcome in Egypt could have been due to their nomadic lifestyle. Hence, they were not perceived as a threat to the Hyksos. However, with the violent expulsion of the Hyksos around 1600 BC, it is entirely possible that the restored native monarchy saw them as threats to national security. Hence, the ominous turn of events in **Exodus 1:8-10,**

- **1:8**, A new king/dynasty came to power. The new "establishment" did not desire to carry on the cordial relationship that existed between Egyptian and the Israelites.

- **1:9-10**, The high Israelite birth rate became a great concern to the Egyptians. The Israelites are viewed as threats to Egypt's national security.

The Pharaoh in question is not named. However, a comparison of this Pharaoh's fear of a growing Israelite population possibly being used as a "fifth column" against the Egyptians stands in stark contrast to the Pharaoh in **Genesis 47:5-6**. A summary of the passage goes like this:

- **47:5,** The king recognizes Joseph and his relatives as a family unit, or "household."

- **47:6,** the family is invited to settle wherever they please. They are even offered positions as livestock keepers.

With the restoration of the native monarchy around 1600 BC, this could have been the reason for the enslavement of the Israelites. The Pharaoh in **Exodus 1:9,** may have been Senakhtenre Tao. He was the African that successfully planned the campaign to oust the Hyksos from Egypt while still exiled in Cush. This may also explain the meaning of the cryptic verse we find in **Genesis 47:6,** which may reflect an old tradition arising from Egypt's post-Hyksos period, that says the "Egyptians despised shepherds" (**Genesis 46:34**).

With the Hyksos removed as a threat around 1670-1600 BC, the Hittites became a problem. The Israelites may have been enslaved in connection to the Hittite threat. The defeat of the Hyksos and the rise of the Hittites may have triggered Egypt's fears concerning the Israelites. This fear of the Israelites may have brought about their enslavement c. 1600 BC. The Egyptians neutralized the Hittites by 1285 BC. The time of the **Exodus** from Egypt is traditionally dated around 1240-1200 BC, this was approximately 40 to 50 years after the Hittites were defeated at the battle of Kadesh-on-the -Orantes River (Syria). With so large a population of non-Egyptians in their midst, this could have caused the Egyptians to classify the Israelites as just as deadly an *internal* threat as the Hittites and Sea People were *external*! Egypt was literally fighting for its life! Hyksos! Hittites! The **Exodus**! Pharaoh lost his fight with the LORD, and the Israelites left Egypt (**Exodus 13-15**). A contingent of Egyptian cavalry drowned in the Sea of Reeds[15] after Pharaoh foolishly sent it to capture the Israelites and return them to slavery. Israel then went free under the leadership of its Egyptian-trained leader, Moses.

Twenty years after the **Exodus,** the Sea Peoples made the first of their two unsuccessful attempts to invade Egypt in 1220 and 1186 BC. At a terrible cost, the Egyptians fought the Sea People to a standstill twice, first in 1220 and then in 1186 BC. The Sea People were expelled, but fled to Canaan. After they settled in Canaan, they built five city-states. They remained a power in the region until David

---

[15]What is translated in English versions of the **Bible** as the *"Red* Sea," is incorrect. The actual area of the deliverance from the Egyptian cavalry is the *Sea of Reeds*. In Hebrew, the body of water that parted for the Israelites was the *Yam Sup,* or *Sea of Reeds*. The scholars that translated the *Septuagint,* for some unknown reason called it the *Red Sea*. Eakin identified the Sea of Reeds with the marshy areas east of Goshen. Goshen was Israel's home during its stay in Egypt. The possible location of the Sea of Reeds may have been either Lake Timsah or Lake Balah. Eakin believed, based upon his reading of **Exodus 13:21**, the LORD supplied a strong wind which exposed a sandbar. This temporary condition allowed the Israelites to literally cross over on "dry land." When the Egyptians attempted to follow the Israelites onto the sandbar, their chariots and horses became mired in the sand. The Egyptian soldiers could have then been thrown from their chariots and trampled by the horses. Those that were not trampled to death were drowned. Frank E. Eakin, Jr., *The Religion and Culture of Israel: An Introduction to Old Testament Thought* (Washington DC: University Press of America, 1977), 63.

absorbed them into his empire around 1000 BC (**2 Samuel 5:17-25**). With the Sea People in Canaan, Egyptian control over that region diminished.

5.7 Chapter Summary

Egypt's technological advantages and its civilized ways both blessed and cursed it. It was blessed, due to its high level of technological advancement, with and a stable society. This stability cursed Egypt because it served as a magnet for the migrating northern tribes.

Egypt's political, economic, and military hegemony which stretched over most of North Africa in the west to Southern Russia in the east, had reached its greatest extent perhaps as early as 4000 BC. From 2100-1200 BC, Egypt's influence and power had been severely curtailed by Aryan tribes that began spilling out of the frozen wastes of Central Asia's Caucasus Mountain Range around 4400 BC.

The Cushite presence in what is known as India was curtailed by a similar horde around the middle Sixteenth Century BC. Between 2400-1750 BC, Mesopotamia was under siege by a different branch of these tribes, the Hurrians. These pressures could have contributed to the massive population shift from Mesopotamia by Cushites like Abraham and his family. This shift caused a steady stream of refugees to flee westward and live a nomadic life in Canaan. By 1670-1600 BC, the Hyksos were expelled from Egypt by a rebellion fomented by an Egyptian commoner, Senakhtenre Tao. It may have also been shortly after the expulsion of the Hyksos that the Black Egyptians turned on the Israelites and viewed them as threats to their national security. The Hittites and Sea Peoples unsuccessfully attempted to conquer Egypt between the Sixteenth and Twelfth Centuries BC. During this time, the Egyptians were trying to keep the Israelites enslaved. Approximately twenty years after the **Exodus**, the Sea People became a threat.

The Hittites and Philistines were crushed by Egyptian force of arms; but at a terrible price, Egyptian control of Canaan was severely curtailed. Egypt, though she remained an influential regional power, would never have the power it had when its empire stretched from Northern Africa to Southern Russia.

An indication of this loss of direct control of Canaan can be seen indirectly by reading the **Biblical** text. As the Israelites invaded Canaan around 1200 BC, the **Scripture** is silent as to any Egyptian attempts to halt their advance under Joshua or to extend their authority over the Israelite settlements (See the books of **Joshua** and **Judges**).

With the departure of the Israelites from Egypt and their eventual occupation of Canaan, this did not mean that they were totally outside of Egypt's sphere of influence. Egypt continued to play an influential part in Israel's existence. King Solomon married an Egyptian princess (**1 Kings 3:1**). This assisted Israel in gaining access to Africa's natural resources and contributing to Solomon's fabled wealth (**1 Kings 10:14-29**).

Egypt would play a part in harboring fugitives from Israelite justice during Solomon's reign (**1 Kings 11:14-40**). After Solomon's death (940 BC), the Egyptians invaded Canaan. Prior to leaving, they burned and sacked Jerusalem (**1 Kings 14:25-26** also **2 Chronicles 12**). **2 Chronicles 14:9** tells of an abortive invasion (c.941 BC) of Judah by a Cushite army, numbering 1,000,000 strong[!] led by their king, Zerah. Pharaoh Necho (609-594 BC) made a vain attempt to reconquer Mesopotamia and in due course was defeated at the battle of Carchemish by King Nebuchadnezzer. Prior to Necho's battle with the Babylonians, King Josiah of Judah foolishly attempted to block the Egyptian advance and died in battle (**2 Chronicles 35:20-24 and 2 Kings 23:28-35**).

Black influence in Egypt was eclipsed by the arrival of the armies of Babylon, led by their king Nebuchadnezzer, in the mid-500s BC. Nebuchadnezzer constructed an empire that stretched from the Tigris and Euphrates Rivers in the East and North Africa in the West. Never again would Egyptian/Cushite influence be felt in the region. By way of these unfortunate occurrences, Egypt would be forever seen as the land portrayed in Cecil B. DeMilles' movie, starring Charlton Heston, *The Ten Commandments*. It would be seen as an ancient land full of splendor and wealth, but populated and dominated by whites.

5.8 Suggestions For Further Reading

Bailey, Randell C. "Is That Any Name for a Nice Hebrew Boy? **Exodus** 2:1-10: The De-Africanization of an Israelite Hero," in, Randell C. Bailey and Jacquelyn Grant, *The Recovery of Black Presence: An Interdisciplinary Exploration* Nashville: Abingdon Press, 1995.

Copher, Charles B. "The Black Presence in the Old Testament," in *Stony The Road We Trod: African-American **Biblical** Interpretation*, ed., Cain Hope Felder, Minneapolis: Augsburg/Fortress Press, 1991.

_____. "Blacks/Negroes: Participants in the Development of Civilization in the Ancient World And Their Presence in the **Bible**," *Journal of the Interdenominational Theological Center, 23:1* (Fall 1995): 3-47.

Morris, Charles A. "The Queen of Sheba and African Matriarchal Precedence," *Journal of the Interdenominational Theological Center*, 19:1/2 (Fall 1991/Spring 1992): 72-87.

Williams, Delores. *Sisters in the Wilderness: The Challenge of Womanist God-Talk.* Maryknoll, NY: Orbis Books, 1993.

Wright, Jr. Jeremiah. *Africans Who Shaped Our Faith :A Study of 10 **Biblical** Personalities*. Chicago: Urban Ministries, 1995.

"Like their co-militarists in all ages, the [African] warriors of the Old Testament could not always accomplish that which they set out to do. They got the better of some battles and the worst of others; they won some wars and were losers of others; that at times staved off invasions, and at some points others prevented them from invading strange lands."

Comments on a failed invasion of Judah by the Cushites under the leadership of their king, Zerah, as recounted in 2 Chronicles 14:9 (941 BC), by The late AME Zion Bishop Alfred G. Dunston, Jr.

CHAPTER 6

Where Do We Go From Here?

Such a simple chapter title! But the answers are not! I suggested a basic idea in this book. I suggested that written documents only take on meaning when they are read and in turn *interpreted*. The document, by itself, has no power. The way it is *interpreted* and in turn *acted upon* is the crucial issue. How the Rabbinical scholars arrived at the conclusion that a) Ham was cursed, and b) certain physical characteristics such as lip size, eye color, hair texture, and skin color, were all marks of this "curse," staggers the imagination. The equation of Black with evil can only be attributed to their being influenced by Aryan beliefs.

We also saw how Christian and Muslim *interpreters* picked up on this Rabbinical theme and used it as an excuse to enslave persons of African descent. However, we also saw how persons of African descent in America *interpreted* the **Bible** for themselves and came to conclusions greatly different than those of the slave masters.

It is the willingness to *interpret* the **Bible** in general and the **Book of Genesis** in particular in an alternative way that will give us a better understanding of our current status as Africans in America. This "status," if we were considered wildlife, (which in essence we are viewed as) would place us on the "endangered species list."

I also suggested that we *re*examine or *re*visit the **Book of Genesis**. By *re*visiting **Genesis**, we were able to suggest that all is not what it seems until other factors are considered. What factors did we consider? We looked at the following points,

- Rather than being considered sub-Human, African people were the *first* Humans. The current level of scientific research considers Africa to be the birthplace of Humanity.

- The **Book of Genesis** and African tradition comes together on several key points concerning the stories of creation, temptation and fall.

- Rather than being cursed, Ham's children populated the world and civilized it.

- Hamitic civilization was sorely tested and curtailed, beginning around 4400 BC, with the advent of Aryan tribes that swept out of the frozen wastes of the Caucasus Mountains.

- The tribes swept east into the region, during the Sixteenth Century BC, now known as "India and disrupted Cushite civilization between 2400-1500 BC. Another wave turned west and disrupted Mesopotamia, thereby causing massive population dislocations. This may have included people such as Abraham, who may have been forced to migrate to Canaan to escape the devastating impact of Aryan infiltration into his native region.

- Egypt went through its "Time of Troubles," it spent nearly five hundred years at war with the Hyksos, Hittites, and the Sea Peoples (1750 and 1180 BC). It is understandable why they may have seen the Israelites living in their midst as national security risks.

- Finally, the LORD freed the Israelites from slavery. This occurred around 1240 BC. They were, for all intents and purposes, Africans. They entered Egypt by way of Jacob/Israel numbering seventy. They left North Africa for Canaan 430 years later, numbering well over a half million. This suggests that they intermarried with the Black population of Egypt. Their leader, Moses was so Africanized that Stephen, an early leader of the Jerusalem Church, states "Moses was trained in all of the wisdom of the Egyptians."

When we add these points together, what do we get? We can arrive at the following conclusions. **Biblical** texts must be *interpreted* in their entirety and that no one commentator, even this one, has the final word on what the text *actually* means. The **Scripture** must be *interpreted* in the light of the latest finds in **Biblical**, scientific, anthropological, historical scholarship and African traditional sources. We must also take seriously the cultural lenses we use to *interpret* the **Bible**. However, we can safely say what the **Bible** does not say. It does *not* claim that *Black-skinned people are inferior*. It does not even say that *white skinned people are inferior*.

Second, since the tradition of African inferiority is so engrained in Western culture, and its Jewish, Christian, and Muslim manifestations, African people must understand that their existence is always tenuous. They will never "arrive." If one segment of Humanity is "cursed," then it would seem that they are *less* than Human. If they are less than Human, then *anything* can be done to them. They can be enslaved, poked, prodded, injected, and experimented upon with impunity. This includes those of us that work in the "Big House," as well as in the "fields." This is what makes such books as *The Bell Curve* so frightening. Why? Because such books, as with the writings of such highly "respected" scientists as Schockley, can be *interpreted* as *written* license to perform unspeakable acts upon African people. These acts will always be done in the name of "the advancement of science," or "national security."

The so-called "curse" placed upon Ham is an excellent example of this. It started with a group of misinformed Fourth Century AD Rabbis and wormed its way into American social policy.

A close examination of the status of Africans in America suggests that racism, as we have experienced it, springs from the so-called "curse" placed upon Ham. The mythology of the "curse" has broken away from its "**Biblical**" moorings and taken on a life of its own. We could even say that the "curse," with its relationship to African "inferiority," has left the realm of religion and taken on the trappings of being a scientific "fact." Renowned African educator, Horace Mann Bond noted in 1934,

> Jefferson Davis [the first and last president of the Confederate States of America] argued against the education of [Africans] on the basis of their inferiority and enforced his argument by *quoting* the *Holy Scripture*; and our present day contemporaries who would limit the education of [Africans] on the basis of their alleged mental inferiority and quote *intelligence tests* as the foundation of their opinion, are [his] spiritual descendents [Italics Added].[1]

Remember Bond's words the next time you hear complaints about "unqualified" minorities (i.e., Africans) getting "preferential" treatment via affirmative action at the expense of "qualified" non-minorities.[2]

---

[1] Horace Mann Bond, *The Education of the Negro in the American Social Order* New York: Prentice-Hall, Inc., 1934; reprint ed., New York: New Octagon Books, Inc.1966), 307.

[2] The February 13, 1995 issue of the conservative leaning *U.S. News and World Report*, published an article that apparently reflects the feeling of many whites, who feel they are being "cheated," by affirmative action programs. The story was entitled, "Affirmative Action on the Edge: A Divisive Debate Begins Over Whether Women and Minorities Still *Deserve* Favored Treatment." The magazine's cover ran the following headline, "Does Affirmative Action Mean, No *White Men* Need Apply? The Battle Over Race and Gender Preferences." [Italics added].

The greater question is, where do we go from here? People of African descent cannot avoid the question. No amount of hiding behind the paper-thin words of a Constitution, which enshrined our "inferiority" will help us. Our people have fought in every armed engagement America has involved itself in, from the first popular riots against British rule in Boston (1770) to the Gulf War (1990). Despite our sacrifices on the "field of valor," we have never been truly accepted as full participants in the American "experience." Why? Because we are still looked upon as being "cursed."

We are the heirs to African *civilization,* not a *curse.* We are also the victims of a *misinterpretation* of the **Bible** based upon the color of our skin. Because of this, it would behoove the African Church in America to be ever more vigilant in its traditional role of *reinterpreting* the **Bible** in such a way as to *liberate* our people. This will only happen when we *deliberate* or discuss the **Bible** in our churches and homes.

Finally, it means that the African Church in America must revisit its traditional role of providing alternative *interpretations* of the **Bible** that defy the dehumanizing patterns of traditional beliefs that see us in a negative light. This also means that the African preacher in America must *revisit* his role as an *interpreter* of the **Scriptures** to those for whom "hope unborn has died." As we face a new millenium, this is a must! This means to read and study the **Bible** in such a way as to have our people and community paraphrase the words of the slave preacher and say, "We—we are not niggers!!!! We—we are not slaves, we are God's Children."

Appendix A

COURSE TITLE: From Eden to Egypt: The Book of Genesis and Africa Revisited

COURSE INSTRUCTOR: Dr. Michael S. Williams

COURSE DURATION: November 12, 1997 through December 17, 1997

COURSE LOCATION: St. James Baptist Church

COURSE DESCRIPTION:
This course seeks to reexamine the **Book of Genesis** in light of its relationship to Africa. First, we will look at **Genesis** and see how it has been historically used against Black People. Second, we will look at the role African people played in God's desire to save the Human Race, (John 3:16).

I. **COURSE DESCRIPTION:**

- Attendance: At least Three Sessions
- Participation: Individual and Group
- Reading Assignments: Do Assigned Reading
- Primary: Brain Usage

II. **RECOMMENDED TEXT BOOKS:**
Bishop Alfred G. Dunston, Jr., *The Black Man in the Old Testament and its World*. Trenton, New Jersey: Africa World Press, 1992.

The Holy Bible

III. **LESSON SCHEDULE:**
- Wednesday, November 12, 1997, Course Introduction
- Wednesday, November 19, 1997, The Location of the **Garden of Eden** and the Origin of the Human Race, **Genesis** 2: 4-25, 3:1-24
- Wednesday, December 3, 1997, **Africa** and the **Table of Nations, Genesis** 10:1-32
- Wednesday, December 10, 1997, **Egypt** and the **Patriarchs, Genesis** 12: 10-14, 37-50

REMEMBER:

THINK!!!!!

Appendix B

The White Man's Burden
By
Rudyard Kipling

Take up the White Man's burden—
    Send forth the best ye breed—
Go bind your son's to exile
    To serve your captive's need;
To wait, in heavy harness,
    On fluttered folk and wild—
Your new-caught sullen peoples,
    Half devil and half child.

Take up the White Man's burden—
    In patience to abide,
To veil the threat of terror
    And check the show of pride;
By open speech and simple,
    And hundred times made plain,
To seek another's profit
    And work another's gain.

Take up the White Man's burden—
    The savage wars of peace—
Fill full the mouth of Famine,
    And bid the sickness cease;

And when your goal is nearest
    (The end for others sought)
Watch sloth and heathen folly
    Bring all your hope to naught.

Take up the White Man's burden
    No iron rule of kings,
But toil of serf and sweeper—
    The tale of common things.
The ports ye shall not enter,
    The roads ye shall not tread,
Go, make them with your living
    And mark them with your dead.

Take up the White Man's burden,
    And reap his old reward—
The blame of those ye better
    The hate of those ye guard—
The cry of host ye humour
    (Ah slowly!) towards the light—
"Why brought ye us from bondage,
    Our loved Egyptian night?"

Take up the White Man's burden—
    Ye dare not stoop to less—
Nor call too loud on Freedom
    To cloak your weariness.
By all ye will or whisper,
    By all ye leave or do,
The silent sullen peoples
    Shall weigh your God and you.

Take up the White Man's burden!
    Have done with childish days—
The lightly proffered laurel,
    The easy ungrudged praise:
Comes now, to search your manhood
    Through all the thankless years,
Cold, edged with dear-brought wisdom
    The judgement of your peers.

Appendix C

Now with regard to mere human matters, the accounts that they gave, and in which all agreed, were the following. The Egyptians, they said, were *the first* to discover the solar year, and to portion out its course into twelve parts. They obtained this knowledge from the stars. To my mind they [construct] their year much more [intelligently] than the Greeks, [for the Greeks add an extra month to the year, every other year, and in due course end up with a 13 month year every other year], *but the Egyptians, dividing the year into twelve months of thirty days each, add every year a space of five days besides, whereby the circuit of the seasons is made to return with uniformity*). [Italics Added]

Appendix D

Medicine is practiced among them on a plan of separation; each physician treats a single disorder, and no more: thus the country swarms with medical practitioners, some undertaking to cure diseases of the eye, others of the head, others again of the teeth, others of the intestines, and some those which are not local.

Appendix E

Sesostris I (ruled Egypt 1980-1926 BC) [marched through] the whole continent of Asia [modern day Turkey], whence he passed on into [Southern] Europe, and made himself master of Scythia [in the area of the Black Sea] and of Thrace [also in the area of the Black Sea], beyond which countries I do not think that his army extended its march. Returning to Egypt from Thrace, he came, on his way, to the banks of the river Phasis. Here I cannot say with any certainty what took place. Either he of his own accord detached a body of troops from his main army and left them to colonize the country, or else a certain number of his soldiers, wearied with their long wanderings, deserted, and established themselves on the banks of this stream.

There can be no doubt that the Colchians* *are an Egyptian race*. Before I heard any mention of the fact from others, I had remarked it myself. After the thought had struck me, I made inquiries on the subject both in Colchis and in Egypt, and I found that the Colchians had a more distinct recollection of the Egyptians, than the Egyptians had of them. Still the Egyptians said that they believed the Colchians to be descended from the army of Sesostris. *My own conjectures were founded, first, on the fact that they are black-skinned and have woolly hair*, which certainly

---
* Ancient Colchis shares the same location as the modern day Republic of Georgia in the former Soviet Union. It is south of the Caucasus Mountain Range and borders the Black Sea. Its wealth was legendary. Colchis is where Jason and his Argonauts traveled to obtain the "Golden Fleece."

amounts to but little, since several other[!] nations are so too; but further and more especially, on the circumstance that the Colchians, the Egyptians, and the [Cushites], are the only nations who have practiced circumcision from the earliest times. The Phoenicians and the Syrians of Palestine themselves confess that they learned the custom of the Egyptians; and the Syrians who dwell about the rivers Thermodon and Parthenius, as well as their neighbors the Macronians, say that they have recently adopted it from the Colchians.

A Response to *From Eden to Egypt: The Book of Genesis Revisited*, by Rev. John Brinson, M.Div.

Dr. Michael S. Williams has written a most important commentary on the **Book of Genesis**. Its importance derives, in part, from the fact that it can serve as a catalyst for a *reinterpretation* of the **Book of Genesis**, especially for Christians of *African* descent. Dr. Williams re*interprets* **Genesis** and draws on factual evidence presented by modern science, the **Bible**, and scholars, both ancient and modern. He draws upon the above named sources and paints a portrait that is both glorious and frightening concerning Humanity's origin in general and that of the African in particular. His book is a glorious effort because he painstakingly weaves a tapestry that demands the African experience be re*interpreted*.

From Eden to Egypt: The Book of Genesis Revisited demands this re*interpretation*. His evidence suggests that Humanity, as we know it, *originated* in *Africa*. Combining the disciplines of Anthropology, History and **Biblical Studies**, he points to the Garden of Eden's location being none other than Africa!

He draws upon a myriad of sources and arrives at the conclusion that African Humanity has been under attack ever since the Ice Age ended several thousand years ago. As the Ice Age ended around 12,000 BC, nomadic tribes, renowned for their blood lust and savagery, began spilling out of Europe towards those areas of the world that had been civilized by the family of Ham. Dr. Williams also uncompromisingly puts forward the glories of African civilization. This portrait is frightening because, using information from African, as well as non-African sources, it shows without a shadow of a doubt why the color "Black" is thought of as evil—*even unto this day*!

Since Dr. Williams "lacks" the "credentials" of a "recognized" **Biblical** scholar, there are two issues that are problematic concerning *From Eden to Egypt: The Book of Genesis Revisited*. First, because of its intent on destroying the images and conclusions held by American society, *From Eden to Egypt: The Book of Genesis Revisited* is seditious and dangerous. Second, it is likely that this book will draw the attention of "Massa" and his loyal band of "House Slaves." I hope that this book will cause even the most loyal of "House Slaves" to reevaluate their position with "Massa" before it's too late!

This book is seditious and disruptive in its proclamation of suppressed information on the **Book of Genesis**. Its seditiousness arises out of its revolutionary intent, which is the liberation of African people, history and images from mainstream theologians, both Caucasian and "colored," who dine at the table of the oppressor. If, as Dr. Williams implies, America is nothing more than a huge plantation and that nothing an African can "do" will ever make him/her palatable to the "powers that be," then, if nothing, Dr. Williams is a "Field Slave" and not a "House Slave." Many that read this book would object to this characterization and protest that such an analysis is archaic, backward and very much *un*-Christian. They will smugly assume that their "privileged" position in "Massa's" House makes them immune to racist "games" or the "Curse of Ham." They will mentally wave their positions in the national (in)security apparatus, their security clearances, their corporate "partnerships," their "corner offices," their positions in business and industry, their being the "first Negro" to... in the face of this work! Caesar had his Brutus, Jesus had His Judas, George Washington had his Benedict Arnold, and the Native Americans had Indian guides that assisted in the slaughter of their brethren by the US Cavalry. The Jews had their "Kapos" in the Nazi concentration camps. Africans in America have historically suffered the betrayal of the "House Slave." The "House Slave" wore "Massa's old clothes and was able to gleefully suck the meatless bones tossed to them from "Massa's" table. They were/are the one's that will look at a book like *From Eden to Egypt: The Book of Genesis Revisited* and seek to "score some points" with "Massa." They just don't understand that after their task has been accomplished, at the end of the day, they are still just "slaves." And sadly enough, they will be surprised when they find out to their horror that slaves that outlive their "usefulness" *can* and *will* be *"dealt with."**

---

[*] I predict that many "Negroes" will protest my views. I invite my misguided brothers and sisters to review the works of the walking wounded and/or disillusioned persons of African descent. I will list a few. Paul M. Barnett, *The Good Black: A True Story of Race in America* New York: E.P. Hutton, 1999), Joseph Jett, *Black and White on Wall Street: The Untold Story of the Man Wrongly Accused of Bringing Down Kidder Peabody* (New York: William Morrow and Company, Inc., 1999), Deborah A. Watts, *101 Ways to Know You're Black in Corporate America* Plymouth, MN: Watts-

In this boldly painted tapestry of information on ancient African history, the Garden of Eden and Egypt, Dr. Williams proceeds from Omo Valley and Olduvia Gorge in East Africa to Egypt. With wide and deliberate brush strokes Dr. Williams provides glances at the history of the barbarian tribes as they swarmed out of Central and Northern Europe and in a systematic manner raped, looted and pillaged the civilized world. He is bold in his claims of Egyptian contributions and influence on the ancient world and consequently on the **Book of Genesis**.

I have read several books on Africans and the people of the **Bible**. Those books were written by very capable African scholars and have learned much from all of them! However, Dr. Williams delves into the subject with a rather different agenda and provides much food for further thought. Like a surgeon he skillfully removes the cancerous myth of the "Curse of Ham." And by implication perhaps discloses the reason the early Rabbis created this myth. This book was written while the "Chosen People" were in captivity and appears to be an attempt at self-glorification and denigration of their former African (Egyptian) hosts.

Dr. Williams has provided us with a seminal tool to assist us in our re*interpretation* of the **Book of Genesis**. I think the major importance of this book is bound up with the revolutionary challenge to Christians of African descent

---

Five Productions, 1998) and Tyrone Power's *Eyes to My Soul: The Rise or Decline of a Black FBI Agent* (Dover, MA: The Majority Press).

to re*interpret* the Christian **Bible** so that it truly becomes the "Gospel" (liberating information) for the oppressed.

If you are of African descent actually living in Africa or living elsewhere in the World, you need to *read* this book. *Buy* it or *borrow* it, but by all means *read* it and *discuss* it with others and it will raise and expand your **Biblical** knowledge and *Christian* consciousness.

Rev. John D Brinson, M/Div.
Clergyman and Author of *Reparations: We Must Demand What Is Due Us*

About the Author

Pastor Michael S. Williams is a native of San Francisco, California. He is a product of San Francisco's public school system. He received his Bachelor of Arts degree *cum laude*, from Bishop College, formerly of Dallas, Texas, in 1976. He earned the Masters of Divinity and Doctor of Ministry degrees from the world-renown Pacific School of Religion, Berkeley, California in 1979 and 1996 respectively.

He served as the Assistant to the President of the Graduate Theological Union from 1996-1997 and holds dual membership with the American Academy of Religion and the Society of **Biblical** Literature. He also belongs to the Middle East Studies Association of North America. Pastor Williams holds the rank of Professor of **Biblical** Studies and Vice President for Development at the Southern Marin **Bible** Institute.

Pastor Williams has been in parish ministry for over a quarter century. He is a respected leader within his denomination, the National Baptist Convention, USA, Inc. and has served in a variety of pastoral and staff positions within the United Methodist Church, the African Methodist Episcopal Zion Church, the National Baptist Convention of America, and the National Baptist Convention, USA, Inc. He currently serves as Pastor of the Saint James Missionary Baptist Church of San Francisco, and Moderator of the Bay Area Baptist District Association.

Pastor Williams is married to the former Patricia A, Andrews. They are the parents of two children, Marthaa and Timothy.

www.ingramcontent.com/pod-product-compliance
Lightning Source LLC
Chambersburg PA
CBHW051939160426
43198CB00013B/2222